think do show

The agile 2.0 secrets to building software people love to use

SIMON EDWARDS

RETHINK PRESS

First published in Great Britain 2019
by Rethink Press (www.rethinkpress.com)

© Copyright Simon Edwards

Dedicated to my beloved father – happy fishing Dad – and to my wonderful mother. Truly loving and supportive parents that every child deserves.

For my princesses, Lili Mae and Evangeline, from your ever loving and incredibly proud Dad.

Contents

Preface   ix

Introduction   1

  My story   1

  Who this book is for   4

  Why you should read this book   7

  How to read this book   10

SECTION ONE THINK   13

ONE Minimum Viable Product Statement   15

  MVP vs MVPS   18

  Why is an MVPS important?   19

  How to build an MVPS that SERVEs   23

  Summary   29

TWO Minimum Viable Product Maps   **31**

What are MVP maps and why are
they important?   32

How to create an MVP map   36

Workshop structure   38

Workshop sample timeline   44

Update your MVP map   45

How to measure your MVP   45

Summary   49

THREE Sprint Schedule   **51**

Why project plans can be
sub-optimal (at best)   52

Timeboxing   56

Introducing sprint schedules   62

Summary   65

FOUR Creating Winning Proposals   **67**

Key elements of a winning proposal   68

Proposal template   70

Summary   74

SECTION TWO DO   **75**

FIVE Setting Up Your Organisation's Structure For Success   **77**

The fallacy of the great idea   77

Communication across an organisation   81

Summary   91

SIX How To Build Effective Agile Functional Teams   **93**

Creating functional agile teams   94

Key roles of functional agile teams   94

Managing the team   103

Motivating the team   105

Pep talks   106

Summary   108

SEVEN The Importance Of Tribes   **109**

What a tribe is and why you need one   109

How to create a tribe and keep it engaged   113

Summary   115

EIGHT Agile Rituals   **117**

Why the agile rituals are so important   118

Agile boards   120

Sprint length   122

Sprint planning 124

Planning poker and story points 129

User stories – best practice 133

The daily stand-up 139

Retrospectives 143

Summary 147

SECTION THREE SHOW **149**

NINE Communicate **151**

Trust 153

TEN How To Give Demonstrations That Rock **155**

Demos and confirmation bias 156

Demo template 158

Demo best practice 161

Summary 166

ELEVEN The One-Page Report **167**

Elements in the report 169

Summary 176

Conclusion **177**

Acknowledgements 183

The Author 187

Preface

A man in a hot air balloon realised he was lost. He reduced his altitude and spotted a woman below. He descended further and shouted out, 'Excuse me, can you help me? I promised a friend I would meet him an hour ago, but I don't know where I am.' The woman below replied, 'You're in a hot air balloon hovering approximately 30 feet above the ground. You're between 40 and 41 degrees north latitude and between 59 and 60 degrees west longitude.' 'You must be in IT,' said the balloonist. 'I am, but how did you know?' asked the woman. 'Well,' answered the balloonist, 'although everything you told me is technically correct, I have no idea how to make sense of your information, and, quite frankly, I'm still lost. You've been no help whatsoever and, if anything, you've actually delayed me.'

The woman below replied, 'You must be in business management.' 'I am, but how did you know?' asked the balloonist. 'Well,' said the woman, 'you don't know where you are or where you're going. You have risen to where you are on a large quantity of hot air. You made a promise that you've got no idea how to keep, and now you expect people beneath you to solve your problems. Quite frankly, you are in exactly the same position you were in before we met, but now, somehow, it's my bloody fault!'

I love that joke. Not because it's hilariously funny – it isn't really funny at all – but because it typifies the feelings of mistrust between the software development team and the business.[1] I've been fortunate to have worked extensively in both camps, so I can empathise with both points of view.

If you're part of a software development team, I suspect that you suffer from the following frustrations most days:

- You're under financial and resource constraints – there's never enough time, money or people to do what someone else has promised you'll do

---

1   In this book I will refer to anyone involved in the actual creation of software as the 'software development team' and anyone involved in defining the requirements, sales, marketing, project management etc of the software as the 'business'.

- Senior management expectations are totally out of whack with what you can and can't get done because the senior managers simply don't understand the pressures you're under

- The business has failed to identify and analyse any risk involved in the project and won't listen to you when you try to highlight it

- There's been a total lack of planning activities to drive the project through to completion and little consideration given to any meaningful form of testing

- Communication about requirements and clarity on roles and responsibilities have been non-existent

- There's been very poor scoping – either too little for the product to make sense, or, more often, too wide a scope for the project even to be delivered, and too much is wanted too soon

- There's been no clearly defined outcome, so you don't know what you're building and why you're building it

- Despite your best attempts to present the business with a realistic picture, it has underestimated the level of integration required; requirement definers simply keep saying, 'Why can't you just plug this into that?'

If, however, you're on the business side of the equation, I suspect that you suffer from the following frustrations:

- Like the software developers, you're under financial and resource constraints

- You've got a limited time frame and budget with which to get a long list of stuff done, and the software development team keeps coming up with ridiculous estimates for the simplest pieces of work – why does everything take so long and cost so much?

- None of the software development team members seem to want to take ownership for the issues we're all facing; there's no responsibility and accountability. (You're accountable to the board for profit and loss, so why aren't they accountable too?)

- You can never understand anything they say – they tell you one thing then totally contradict themselves by saying something else

- The software developers can't seem to explain things in a way that you can actually understand so that you can help them resolve issues

- It is all so complicated – it's only software; it can't be that hard

- You spend hours telling the software developers what you want, and then it takes them forever to deliver something completely different from what you asked for

In essence, the software development team is per-ceived as not understanding the business: 'They don't deliver. They never give us what we want. They cost too much.' The business is perceived as not under-standing the software development team: 'They don't know what they want. They keep changing their minds. They demand too much; we don't have the resources.'

Sadly, this degree of confusion and mistrust tends to characterise the relationship between the software development teams and the business. But this is not everyone's experience; there is a better way...

Introduction

My story

Delivering software that people love to use is one of the most rewarding things you can do with your life. Great software that is well designed and offers a beautifully simple user experience which solves specific problems has the ability to transform people's lives.

Working with a dedicated, committed team of people who are passionate about their users' needs and work hand in hand with the business is an absolute joy. People outside our industry believe that software development and code is all about complex maths and algorithms when in reality it's not – software development is a highly creative, problem solving skill.

Developing innovative, simple and elegant solutions to people's everyday issues is huge fun too. If, like me, you love the whole end-to-end lifecycle then it's no longer work as such but a passion that you have.

In my career, I've worked and been able to learn in so many industries, ranging from telecommunications, mobile, pharmaceuticals, oil and energy to banking, investments, transport, policing and even nuclear defence. I've met some truly amazing people and collaborated with industry experts, product owners and development teams to transform people's working lives and enable them to greatly improve the value of their work. It's been a fantastic journey and a real honour.

But it wasn't always like this for me. For a long time, I suffered from the same frustrations that you probably face every day. I started my career at the UK telecommunications giant BT Plc, in business operations, dealing with the day-to-day running of the business and the product line. In 2005, I was working with our IT department on a suite of software applications to manage the rollout of global customer networks in conjunction with the internet conglomerate Cisco Systems. The IT industry was very much waterfalled then, and I just couldn't understand why our IT department would spend so much time planning, creating huge tomes of documents and not really writing much code. I got so frustrated that I decided to join them to see what was going on. So I trained as a technical business analyst and then as a developer. It quickly became apparent that I wasn't a very good programmer, but the exposure over a couple of years to the technical aspects of development meant that I had a unique perspective. I'd worked with and had experience of both sides of the fence and so was able to fully understand and appreciate the issues of the two disciplines: business and software development.

Around this time I met Ken Schwaber, who gave a talk about the 'agile' methodology at BT Labs Martlesham. BT's R&D centre gave the world a number of techno-logical inventions such as fibre optics, cellular data, IPX (Internetwork Packet Exchange) and QKD (quantum key distribution). Ken was travelling the world touting the *Agile Manifesto*,[2] which he and his fellow collaborators had penned a few years earlier. I was in awe of Ken; everything he said made so much sense to me and he was willing to freely share his knowledge and wisdom.

I was desperate to implement this radical new way of working, but, sadly, the senior executives weren't so enthusiastic to abandon their ingrained ways of working, even though they clearly weren't working. Luckily for me, I happened upon a progressive young

---

2   Kent Beck, Mike Beedle, Arie van Bennekum, Alistair Cockburn, Ward Cunningham, Martin Fowler, James Grenning, Jim Highsmith, Andrew Hunt, Ron Jeffries, Jon Kern, Brian Marick, Robert C Martin, Steve Mellor, Ken Schwaber, Jeff Sutherland, and Dave Thomas, *Manifesto For Agile Software Development* (2001). http://agilemanifesto.org

executive, Jason Cook, who would go on to become the chief architect for BT Americas, and my dear friend to this day. Jason gave me a small development team, free rein to do as I pleased, and air cover from the rest of the business and the IT department. In ninety short days we shipped an internal app in conjunction with Cisco that would process the order of routers and switches for customer networks. In the first two years of operation the web app processed four billion dollars in order value, won an innovation award at New York City's investment and securities expo 'SIFMA' in 2007, and was a huge favourite among users. The reason we were so successful was that we concentrated on fixing one problem only and fixing it well from a user's perspective.

While I stumbled my way through the first few projects, the basic principles remained the same. I continued to learn, perfect and hone the agile techniques until I distilled them into the 'secrets' that you will learn from this book.

Who this book is for

Every time I sat down to write a part of this book I put up two photos next to my writing desk. They were stock photos that I downloaded from the internet of stressed, frustrated professionals. For me, one represented the business operations side of an organisation and the other represented their counterpart from the software development team.

When I wrote each section I envisaged both viewpoints and drew from my experience, having worked extensively in both disciplines. I would think to myself: 'What are the specific needs and problems that the business-focused person faces, and, likewise, what are they for their software development counterpart?' This book is very much about bringing both disciplines together for the benefit of all. It's about building a common language that all parts of the organisation can understand and get value from, whatever the individuals' specific needs. The business cannot survive in this information age without the support of an onboard IT department, and an IT department doesn't exist without the business to support it. Successful companies like Apple, Google and Spotify happily marry the two.

If, for example, you're a frustrated, stressed-out product owner from the business, or if you're an equally frustrated, stressed-out development lead, then this book was written for you, to help solve your problems and to help you work much more productively with your colleagues. Equally, if you're a senior executive who just can't get to the bottom of why product delivery is taking so long then I hope you too benefit greatly from this book.

Maybe your company has started down the agile route and you haven't ended up at the promised land you were led to believe in. For me, agile is an empowering, beautifully elegant and simple framework in which people can freely express themselves and do their finest work. I refuse to work in any other environment. However, I suspect that's not most people's experience of agile. When I'm asked to consult for organisations who euphemistically call themselves 'agile practitioners', I encounter something very different from the talk I heard Ken Schwaber give back in 2005. The industry seems to have taken agile and made it so overtly complex and process-driven that it no longer represents the vision of its founders but some behemoth monster out of control. If this is your experience, then in this book we'll get back to basics and rediscover the magical simplicity of agile working.

I suspect the reason most organisations have so many issues adopting agile has to do with the current illusion of control and certainty and the organisations' total reticence to let go of something that clearly isn't working. Because the company has a project plan and because it has forecast costs which look about right, then it assumes that everything is OK and is gonna work out fine. But clearly, given the Harvard research, which I explain more in the next section, and countless other studies which echo the same conclusion, everything isn't OK and isn't gonna work out fine. Yet senior executives still cling to their precious project plans that forecast the future like a cheap horoscope in the daily tabloids.

To do agile properly you have to go all in. As my beloved late father used to tell me, 'Decide to do something properly, son, or don't bother at all'. Senior executives need to truly empower their employees and trust them to do the job properly. This book addresses these senior executives' issues too, so that they can start to feel comfortable letting go of their out-of-date illusions.

Why you should read this book

Are you confident that your organisation or team delivers amazing software that people love to use? If you are, then please put this book down and carry on doing what you're doing because it's obviously working.

Or is your experience of the whole software delivery lifecycle a bit more like this: You feel that there seems to be no agreement about what problem the software is actually trying to solve and, more importantly, why you're trying to solve it. It's as if the business and the IT department have completely different agendas that are at odds with each other, and that the customer and user community certainly isn't at the centre of either of those agendas. Does it feel like there's little understanding and partnership between the business and

IT departments, that there's most definitely insufficient ownership and accountability over the problem space or delivering software on time? Your business has constraints on time, resources, skilled people and budgets. Have you noticed poor communication between the business and IT departments, leading to a total lack of transparency and trust? Is no one in your organisation thinking about shared outcomes and the impact of the software being produced on your users and your customers? Do you feel that the boat just isn't going fast enough and there's too much at stake for you to fail?

If this is your experience then don't despair, because you're definitely not alone. A study published in the *Harvard Business Review*[3] analysed 1,471 IT projects and found that on average the overrun across all projects was nearly a third. More damning, however, was that one in six projects ended up costing four times the original quote and on average took more than two thirds more time than had been estimated at the start. So the second scenario I described above seems to be the norm rather than the exception.

In this book I will show you easy-to-follow techniques that will enable you to:

---

3   Bent Flyvbjerg and Alexander Budzier, 'Why Your IT
    Project May Be Riskier Than You Think', *Harvard Business
    Review* (September 2011). https://hbr.org/2011/09/
    why-your-it-project-may-be-riskier-than-you-think

- Create a simple, commonly agreed statement about what software you're building and why

- Map out only the features you need to solve the problem(s) you're trying to solve

- Put those features onto a schedule that everyone can understand

- Set up a crusading team who will cut swiftly through the corporate fog to ship real software

- Crank the delivery arm faster than ever

- Show everyone your amazing work and build a tribe of passionate followers and supporters

- End micro management and 'death by a thousand reports'

I honed and perfected the 'secret' techniques in this book over several years, working with many global corporations such as Cisco, Microsoft, BT Plc and Telefonica; they were even used to launch the iPhone in the UK for O2, in conjunction with some amazing talent at Apple.

The techniques have also transformed the way criminal justice is administered in London, saving hundreds of thousands of hours of police, court and lawyer time, and, as of the time of writing, the techniques are being used at the MoD in London to develop a response system in case of a nuclear weapons or reactor incident. (Let's hope we never have to use that system, though!) Can you imagine what these techniques could help your company do?

How to read this book

This book isn't an agile start-up guide. There are hundreds of books out there introducing agile, and I certainly didn't want to add to that already-existing body of knowledge. I assume you've had some experience of agile – probably negative, hence you reading this book. If you would like to read a primer, then I'd certainly recommend the excellent and free Scrum guide written by Jeff Sutherland and the above-mentioned Ken Schwaber.[4]

I wanted to write a book with accessible ideas, useful stuff that you can dip into and take away and act on today. Getting you to read a book and not act on it is like opening a cocktail bar and filling it with teetotallers. It's a waste of everyone's time.

The book is split into three main sections, named Think, Do and Show. The Think section is all about effective planning and discovering your 'why'. I introduce you to some new concepts and techniques such as MVPS, MVP maps and the sprint schedule, which will help you clearly articulate what it is you're building, why you're building it and the fastest route

---

4   Ken Schwaber and Jeff Sutherland, 'The Scrum Guide' (2018). www.scrumguides.org/scrum-guide.html

to get it built. The Do section is all about cranking the delivery arm. I introduce you to agile functional teams and talk about how to energise and motivate a team so that it drives itself to guaranteed success. The third section, Show, will teach you all about effective communications within the wider organisation. I introduce the 'one-pager' report and give some valuable tips about one of the most important agile rituals, the demonstration (sometimes referred to as the 'show-and-tell').

I would recommend reading the book in sequence, but if you want some particular guidance or help with any of the three main areas then feel free to jump straight to that section. You will still learn some valuable techniques and 'secrets' which you can put to work straight away.

Now that you're armed with the knowledge of what you will learn from this book, let's get started right away with the Think section and learn how best to plan a successful software delivery.

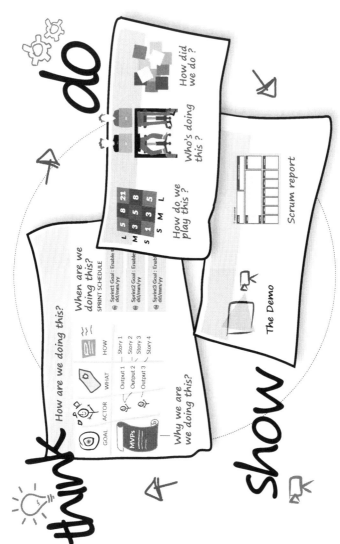

The 'Think, Do, Show' Framework

ONE

Minimum Viable Product Statement

'In preparing for battle, I have always found that plans are useless but planning is indispensable.'
— Dwight D. Eisenhower

When it comes to planning, most people fall into two distinct camps: those from the traditional PRINCE2- and waterfall-type backgrounds who want to plan right down to the level of toilet break, and those from a 'We know what we're doing, let's just get on with it' camp who don't bother to plan at all. In this first section of *Think, Do, Show*, we're going to look at the issues with both approaches and then introduce an elegant, pragmatic key to simple and effective planning.

If there's such a thing as 'death by PowerPoint', then there's most certainly an equivalent 'death by project plan'. I could never understand the infatuation that planners, project managers, senior executives and others have with project plans. They always remind me of the *Peanuts* character Linus and his comfort blanket. Because that's all they really are – a comfort blanket.

Some would argue that a project plan is an invaluable, detailed list of activities required to see a project through to success in a timely manner. Is it really? At its basic level a project plan is a guess about the future. Yes, it's an educated guess, based on past experiences and learning, but it's still a guess. The only way to ever write an accurate project plan is to write it after you've delivered the project; only then is it no longer a guess but accurate information. If project plans are so valuable, then why are they updated on a weekly basis with what's really been delivered and achieved? On the flip side, the *Agile Manifesto*'s principle of 'working software over comprehensive documentation'[5] has been misinterpreted by many agile practitioners as a directive to not do any documentation or planning at all. I would suggest that neither approach is truly optimal.

The auto-pilot function on an aeroplane works by knowing where the aeroplane needs to go and when it needs to get there. It then constantly adjusts the

---

5   Beck et al, *Manifesto*.

controls, speed and direction of the aeroplane to take into account constantly changing variables like wind speed, weight and fuel. That's how we need to approach planning: knowing exactly what needs to be delivered and by when, knowing what landmarks and milestones need to reached on the way, and adjusting to the naturally changing landscape that the teams operate in.

We'll open the Think section of the book by introducing the concept of an MVPS. You may have heard of the Lean Delivery model MVP (minimum viable product). I will introduce you to the 'minimum viable product statement' concept. An MVPS is an agreed, common vision statement between the software delivery team and the business. Its purpose is to clearly articulate what you're building and why you're building it. It also becomes a powerful rallying cry for the project and a way to guard against the dreaded scope creep.

We'll use the MVPS as the first building block to an MVP map. An MVP map is a powerful way for the business and software development teams to collaborate on building the initial MVP. In this section, I'll introduce some simple tools for building an MVP with a strong emphasis on the 'viable' and not the 'minimal'. Once the MVP is built and mapped then we'll look at adding measurements to the map that will show us what success looks like.

The Prussian army Chief of Staff Helmuth von Moltke the Elder famously said that 'No plan survives contact with the enemy'.[6] That's why we don't need a plan but rather a map and a compass. Our map and compass will be the sprint schedule, which we'll also look at closely in this section.

Finally, as a bonus, I'll demonstrate a way in which all these powerful planning artefacts can be used to create winning proposals with fixed timelines and budgets that can be presented to decision makers.

In this chapter I'll introduce the concept of an MVPS, the benefits of having one and the common pitfalls of not having one. We'll take a look at how to create a powerful MVPS and the key elements that need to be present, with some real-world examples given along the way. By the end of this chapter you'll be able to create a powerful MVPS that acts as a key point of focus for your project.

MVP vs MVPS

In his international bestseller *The Lean Startup*, Eric Ries first coined the concept of an MVP. Ries described an MVP as follows: 'A Minimum Viable Product is that version of a new product which allows a team to collect the maximum amount of validated learning about

---

6   Von Moltke, 'Ueber Strategie', *Kriegsgeschichtliche Einzelschriften* (1891).

customers with the least effort.'[7] For our purposes, though, an MVP is essentially the smallest thing you can build that delivers customer value.

An MVPS, then, is a single sentence that encapsulates the purpose of the MVP and the desired end result. It should detail precisely the specific value being delivered in either a user scenario or feature form. It should also detail how the delivered value can be measured in some way.

Why is an MVPS important?

A collectively agreed-on MVPS acts as a focal point for a project. All parties involved know what's being delivered and why. The business has a clear understanding of what it's getting, and what it's not getting, and the development team knows what's expected of them, leaving no ambiguity. This actually helps develop trust between both parties, too. With a clearly agreed MVP, all parties become transparently accountable. An MVPS therefore serves the MVP (more on this concept in the next part of this chapter).

An MVPS is also an excellent barometer for which features absolutely need to be present and which ones don't. With an MVPS which clearly states 'Search customer orders', there's no need to add other

---

7   Eric Reis, *The Lean Startup* (2011). http://theleanstartup.com

functionality such as editing and deletion of customer records. These features may or may not come later.

Scope creep is the bane of most delivery teams. And it should also be the bane of all business teams because it tends to inadvertently shift focus away from the business goal. Well-meaning product managers try to cram in new features because they may be cool and trendy or because the competition has them. A good MVP with a specific business value doesn't need scope creep. It needs to focus on the goal at hand and get there as quickly as possible.

Every successful project has a rallying cry, a cause to crusade against and a 'why'. In his excellent book *Start With Why*,[8] Simon Sinek details how the 'why' of a project or product inspires the people involved to achieve remarkable things. Most organisations can explain what a product does or how it works, but it's the why that people really value. A good MVPS provides the why.

How will we know if we've been successful? The only way to do this is to have a clear measurement of success. An MVPS should detail this either implicitly or explicitly. There can be no argument about what success means and how to prove it was – or was not – achieved.

---

8   Simon Sinek, *Start With Why: How great leaders inspire everyone to take action* (2011). https://startwithwhy.com

A PAINFUL LESSON IN NOT HAVING AN MVPS

Before I developed the concept of an MVPS, back in 2011 I worked with a major UK mobile comms provider on the launch of the iPhone 4S. My development team was asked to deliver a 'Register Your Interest' form which could be accessed via existing subscribers' mobile phones, the web and via a Facebook applet. The purpose of the form from the sales team perspective was to generate as many leads as possible so those customers could be better targeted and turned into sales. The purpose from the content team perspective was to gather information that would help them deliver specific content to different user groups. And the purpose from the marketing team perspective was to use the exercise to gather valuable marketing data that it lacked from its existing customers.

With all these different purposes in mind, we delivered a form with thirteen different fields that customers had to complete in order to register interest. The marketing team built a campaign around a ten-day countdown to launch. As it happens, Apple never gave a launch date, so the one in our campaign was a lucky guess based around the upcoming Apple Media Event in October 2011!

On day one of the campaign, the form was released and promoted. There was little take-up of the form. The same was the case on day two. The mobile comms operator was worried because it had many subscribers who were due for an upgrade on their iPhone. Why weren't they showing interest? By day four, there was real concern and a meeting was called with all parties involved and the director of sales and marketing. It's pretty obvious why there was little uptake. Who is going to fill out a 'Register Your Interest' form with thirteen different fields, especially on a mobile device with the web experience of 2011? 'Very few people' was the answer.

At the meeting, the director of sales and marketing clearly stated that retaining and expanding market share was the number-one priority and, therefore, that the form should be as easy as possible to submit. In order to register interest, only a mobile number or an email address was actually required. Consequently, we stripped out every field from the form except the mobile number and email address, making only one of the two mandatory, and shipped the form to production. Predictably, uptake shot up dramatically from then on. After the launch of the iPhone 4S it became obvious that the mobile comms provider had much lower sales than expected and had indeed lost market share. Had we created a clear MVPS stating the business value and intent at the beginning then we would have only shipped with the two fields and potentially avoided loss of market share.

How to build an MVPS that SERVEs

I've developed the acronym SERVE to describe the key elements of an MVPS that describes, or SERVEs, an MVP. I'll detail them now and then share some real-world examples with you.

- **S**ingle business goal – user- or product-specific
- **E**xclusive – delivers business value independently, in and of itself
- **R**ealistic – can be achieved by the development team in a reasonably specified time frame
- **V**aluable – achieves a specific goal / supports the business strategy
- **E**vidential – be measurable, with the ability to prove that it was delivered

Single business goal

The key to successful delivery is to concentrate on a single business goal. Projects tend to be too ambitious and bite off more than they can chew. Organisations are far more likely to be successful if they deliver small projects and then build upon those successes. This is the true meaning of iteration and why it is so powerful. Software project goals are either user- or product-specific. Either they empower a user to do something they weren't able to do before, or to do something they could always do easier, faster and cheaper, or they deliver a new product or product feature. Concentrate on what would add the most value to your organisation at this moment in time. Taking your corporate strategy as a guide, identify the single most urgent or compelling business goal you could achieve right now and concentrate on that.

Exclusive

An MVP must deliver some kind of business value as a single delivery without dependencies which are external to the project. In the real world that's often difficult to achieve, but strive to be as independent as possible or ensure that the team has all the skills it needs to deliver the project (more on this in the Do section). Software reuse in the form of APIs is an absolutely valid option for this.

Realistic

Can we achieve what we're setting out to achieve? The MVP should be as realistically achievable as possible. Always stretch the team, just don't set them up for failure. Completing a series of spikes (mini software investigations/researches) are great for discovering what's realistically achievable. Capturing this in the MVPS gives everyone the confidence that the project can be successfully delivered.

Valuable

For stakeholder management it's vital to ensure that the MVP meets a single goal that is truly valuable to the business, usually in the form of either protecting revenue, generating revenue or reducing costs. If you can articulate this in the MVPS then you'll get greater stakeholder support and know that you are actively contributing to the health of the organisation. If you want true stakeholder engagement, then follow the money.

Evidential

Did we achieve what we set out to achieve? This is the key question following the completion of a project, and the only way to answer it is to have some way of measuring success. This can be explicit – for example, a specific Key Performance Indicator (KPI) measuring factors such as revenue or increased user numbers – or it can be implicit, enabling a user to do something that they couldn't before or delivering a new feature to an existing product.

Now that we've looked at the key elements that an MVPS should encompass, let's look at some real-world examples.

'As an officer I want to present to a decision maker, within a single system, the minimum necessary information, including witness

statements and previous convictions, so that
a charging disposal decision can be made and
recorded within 24 hours.'

The example above was taken from a project to deliver
a powerful criminal justice prosecution system for the
Met Police in London, which is in wide use within the
Met as of the writing of this book. *(You've been warned.)*
Let's break down this example using our SERVE
acronym:

- **S**ingle business goal – 'so that a charging decision
  can be made and recorded': the single goal is to
  enable a supervisor to record a charging decision

- **E**xclusive – 'within a single system': this clearly
  states there are to be no outside dependencies

- **R**ealistic – 'the minimum necessary information,
  including witness statements and previous
  convictions': the exact-scope definition that
  the team had spiked beforehand and were
  comfortable with

- **V**aluable – 'so that a charging disposal decision
  can be made and recorded within 24 hours': this is
  a legal requirement within the framework of the
  UK judiciary service that all UK constabularies
  have to adhere to

- **E**stimable – 'within 24 hours': no arguments there,
  then

'To enable the decommissioning of the ISBE platform, we will deliver a like-for-like replacement of the trade settlement team's ePortal using our existing adopted open-source framework, thereby saving [£x] costs per annum.'

This example was taken from a project to upgrade an investment banking system. The 'ISBE' was a legacy trading platform, costly to maintain and consistently breaking, that needed replacing. Most of the infrastructure had already been swapped out but there was a vital web portal that needed to be replaced before decommissioning could be carried out and business value delivered. Let's break this example down using our SERVE acronym:

- **S**ingle business goal – 'to enable the decommissioning of the ISBE platform'

- **E**xclusive – 'using our existing adopted open-source framework': The bank had adopted a collection of open-source tools. This part of the statement ensured that the development team had the required expertise and knowledge of an existing toolset to carry out the delivery.

- **R**ealistic – 'like-for-like': No *more* features and no *fewer* features. This part of the statement also clearly discourages scope creep.

- **V**aluable – 'thereby saving [£x] costs per annum': a concise, valuable business delivery

- **E**stimable – there are two points of measurement here: 'like-for-like replacement' and 'saving [£x] costs per annum'

And, finally, the last example that I use when coaching and teaching teams, which is my favourite due to its brevity and simplicity. It was written by George Berkowski, author of the Amazon number one bestseller *How to Build a Billion Dollar App*.[9] I had the pleasure of working with George at Hailo on their eHailing app.

'Get a licensed taxi in two taps'

If we were to break this down using SERVE, for each element of the acronym we'd simply repeat 'Get a licensed taxi in two taps'. For example, getting a licensed taxi in only two taps is *valuable* in terms of speed of access to both users and the business. This example clearly shows that an MVPS can be extremely simple, yet powerfully effective. In fact, the marketing team shortened this to the famous strapline that it used on all Hailo marketing at the time: 'Two taps to a taxi'.

---

9   George Berkowski, *How To Build A Billion Dollar App* (2014). www.amazon.co.uk/How-Build-Billion-Dollar-entrepreneurs/ dp/0349401373/ref=sr_1_1?ie=UTF8&qid=1547996395&sr=8-1&keywords=george+berkowski and https://mybilliondollarapp. com/about-george-berkowski

Summary

In this chapter we've been introduced to MVPS, looked at the benefits of having one and examined the pitfalls of not having one. We've also looked at how they're formulated using the SERVE acronym and a few real-world examples. You should now be able to create an MVPS for your own project. I strongly recommend you do this and have both the business and the development team agree on it.

Use your MVPS on all your communications around your project. State it on your reports, on your opening slides to demonstrations and in any wider communications within your organisation (we'll review reports and demonstrations in Section 3: Show). It will act as a powerful reminder to everyone of what your project is about and why it matters.

TWO

Minimum Viable Product Maps

'Our intention creates our reality.'
— Wayne Dyer

In this chapter we're going to build on our MVPS by introducing MVP maps. Essentially, MVP maps detail the 'who', the 'what' and the 'how' necessary to deliver the MVP in the shortest time and with business value. We'll take a look what MVP maps are and why they're important, then we'll introduce the visual element and break down its simple components. Next, we'll look at how to run a workshop where the MVP maps are fleshed out and run through some examples. Finally, we'll review how to add metrics to MVP maps so that we end up with a single-page visual representation of our entire MVP that will ultimately deliver our MVPS.

This is a fantastic artefact to share with the entire business. All interested parties can see, on a single page, what's being delivered, why it's being delivered and metrics to prove that it has indeed been successfully delivered.

What are MVP maps and why are they important?

Traditional requirements documents tend to be merely shopping lists of features, accumulated from various business analyses, all bundled together 'just in case we missed something'. What they lack is any kind of business context as to why, or even if, they're important. There's no clear linkage back to the reason why the business is doing the project in the first place or how each feature directly supports the underlying business value.

Consequently, it's virtually impossible to say whether feature 'x' should be developed and invested in or not. Within any reasonably sized organisation with multiple stakeholders, this results in thick requirements documents with hundreds, if not thousands, of requirements and stakeholder pet features which are totally out of scope with the business objective. If this is how you start a software project, it's pretty clear how it's going to end.

MVP maps negate all this unnecessary detail and pare down deliverables into what's truly required to realise the MVPS. They are a visual collaboration between the business and the delivery team. The entire project team will come together in a workshop to build the map over several iterations. The process usually only takes a day and will save enormous amounts of time and costs during the lifecycle of a project.

An MVP map shows a direct correlation between a feature (referred to as a story), the outputs and the actors responsible for the outputs. It then becomes very clear which stories actually do support the MVPS and which ones don't. This helps us throw out any stories that do not directly contribute to the overall MVPS and drill down to the essentials.

Remember, our goal is always to find the fastest route to the MVPS. The faster we get there and prove our MVP, the cheaper and more efficient we become. Then the business is in a much better position to evaluate the delivery and potentially invest more resources in MVP 2.0, for example, further enhancing the project and delivered business value.

MVP maps also clearly show the reasoning behind a potential story suggestion. Again, this allows us to further scrutinise that reasoning. Someone looking at the map from a different perspective can then challenge the reasoning and assumptions and perhaps come up with better, more efficient ways of creating the outputs required to deliver the MVPS.

Creating an MVP map is a collaborative process where everyone is involved, the output of which is a collective agreement – a collective agreement of what's being delivered, why and who's accountable for each element. Publishing the output is important from a transparency perspective so that no grey areas remain. It's a kind of team declaration of 'this is what we're going to do'.

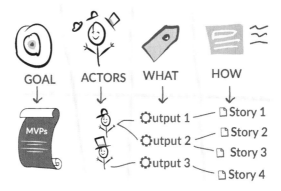

Figure 2.1: MVP Map Structure – outline

An MVP map consists of four columns, where each column branches into the next. The columns are named:

Goal

In this column, you reiterate the MVPS; for instance, from our Hailo example in Chapter 1, this is where we'd simply write, 'Get a licensed taxi in two taps'.

Actor

Here you list the role of individuals who have a direct impact on enabling the MVPS. From our Met Police example in Chapter 1 we would add the roles of the OIC (Officer in Charge) and Supervising Sergeant. When creating this list, avoid the temptation to add the world to the list; try to consider the minimum number of actors necessary. You only want those who can directly impact the outputs required to achieve the MVPS. This is a great opportunity to ask the question, 'Does so and so *really* need to be involved?' Obviously, the fewer handoffs you have in a process the more efficient it becomes.

What

The 'whats' are the outputs required to achieve the MVPS. Think about what artefacts have to be produced; you may consider documents, forms, data that has to be collected, specific actions that have to be carried out and other outputs. Remember that many outputs will be inputs for the next part of the delivery.

How

The 'how' is made up of the specific stories that will go to the delivery team, and the majority of your effort in creating the MVP map during a workshop will be spent drafting these stories. For the purposes of the MVP map, keep the stories at a high level. At this point, these are more placeholder stories for further detail later rather than finalised stories. The stories will be fleshed out in detail during agile planning, and I'll explain more about this in the Do section of the book.

This simple structure provides a great way to convey on a single page what could be a complex delivery. Yes, there will always be more detail behind the MVP map, but this acts as a fantastic helicopter view of the whole project. It can be referenced and referred to in meetings during delivery and used to easily explain the overall rationale behind the delivery to stakeholders, third parties and others. Anyone should be able to look at your MVP map and say, 'Oh, yeah… I get it', and ask relevant, informed questions.

How to create an MVP map

By far, the best way to create an MVP map is to hold a one-off workshop and thrash through it with all interested parties. Whilst it's not within the realm of this book to fully deal with every element of a successful workshop,[10] I will lay out a simple structure that's

---

10 If you are interested in further reading in the areas of meeting facilitation, idea generating and problem solving, then I would recommend *Idea Stormers* by Bryan W. Mattimore (2012), *Gamestorming* by Dave Gray (2010) and *Visual Meetings* by David Sibbet (2010). These books are filled with ideas for generating collaborative working, creating new ideas and mapping out storyboards.

always proved highly successful for any workshops I've facilitated. First, some preliminaries:

Who should attend

My simple rule of thumb here is to include anyone with skin in the game and 'the decider'. By 'skin in the game', I mean anyone who will be directly involved in the actual delivery and is therefore accountable for the delivery. Anyone who's going to physically do the work, not just report on what everyone else is doing. Also try to keep the hierarchy as flat as possible. Everyone at the workshop should be equal with a single goal: to produce the best, most useful MVP map possible. Everyone's voice should be viewed as important, and everyone should be encouraged to contribute. Your project is too important to have shrinking violets at the party and equally too important to have just one person dictate the solution. Reap the wisdom of crowds.

The 'decider' is the primary stakeholder for the project. This should be the person who is ultimately responsible for owning the business value that is to be delivered. Make sure this is a single person and not a collective. You're going to be generating many ideas, viewpoints and rationale – some of which will inevitably clash. Many of these clashes can be negotiated by the team, but at times you will need a single person to turn to and ask, 'Are we doing this, or are we doing that?'

Location

The only key point regarding the location is to make sure you have plenty of space and lots of stationery materials. You can't have enough paper, white boards, flip charts, post-it notes, pens, highlighters, stickers, etc. There's something very playful and tactile about stationery that seems to help people get creative. Make sure that basic needs are taken care of too, such as amenities, food and drink. And ensure that there are no disturbances – mobiles on silent!

Workshop structure

Set the objective

Remind the attendees of the MVPS and why it's important to the business; you may prefer to ask the decider to do this. As it's in their interest to see the project through to fruition, the decider can often speak with great passion regarding the project's importance to the business and to those directly involved in the delivery, thereby energising everyone.

Collectively list the actors

As a group, list the actors involved from the MVPS – who is specifically required to deliver the outputs? With attendees representing the end-to-end delivery, this is a good time to evaluate who is relevant and who isn't. Together, ask questions like, 'Does (x role) really need to be involved?' and 'Can we reduce the number of actors here?' As noted earlier, having the smallest possible number of actors involved means fewer handovers, therefore increasing the efficiency of the process.

Collectively list the outputs

Again, as a group, list all the outputs necessary to deliver the MVPS. Challenge conventional wisdom here – maybe some outputs could be grouped, maybe some could be dropped, perhaps new ones are required or others could be replaced.

Work individually for thirty minutes on the 'how'

It's at this point in traditional workshops where we start the dreaded brainstorming session. I say 'dreaded' because in my experience brainstorming at its best is less than optimal and at its worst is downright damaging. Traditional brainstorming always follows one train of thought and key idea. A member of the team will put forth an idea which garners collective agreement. Then every subsequent idea from the team is a variation on that single thought.

These brainstorming sessions never seem to facilitate original out-of-the-box thinking after the initial key idea. They simply generate variations on a theme. To avoid this in your workshop, get each team member to work individually on their own solution. This empowers the individual's creative freedom as there are no constraints to their thinking. Encourage team members to storyboard their solutions with post-it notes, on a flip chart or using anything else they can to share their ideas with the wider team.

Share and individually review the output

Ask each team member to display their solution on a board or a wall and allow time for the team members to review each other's ideas in isolation. Don't open any debate at this time, just allow some time for team members to absorb each other's ideas. Oddly, this 'alone time' is a very important step in the collaboration process. Allowing individuals this time to process each other's ideas gives them a great context when they come back together to collaborate.

Everyone gets three votes

Allow each team member to vote for their three favourite ideas, suggestions or other contributions from the team. Simply use a pen mark or (my favourite option) give each team member three circular stickers and give them free rein to vote for outputs on the flip charts, post-it notes etc.

Gather the top ideas

Collectively review which ideas seem to be the most popular and write or draw them anew on a wipe board or flip chart. Here you can use whatever notation or scribbling you like best. It doesn't really matter if you use stick figures or simple boxes or whatever. It's not meant to be a work of art, just a visual aid that everyone can relate to and gather around. This rough, sample solution is only the start of your collaborative exercise.

Iterate through to an agreed solution

Collectively review the sample solution and work through it to an agreed final proposal. The final proposal should take the form of the outputs (the whats) and the stories (the hows). It's important at this point to restate that the objective is to find the fastest route to the MVPS and to map out one clear happy path. At this point in the project it's impossible to map out every eventuality, every point where the process could break down or need reversing or amending. There will be some who will say: 'But what if this happens, and what if that happens?' but it's best to avoid the 'what if' brigade for now. Healthy, challenging debate is good and should be encouraged, but there's a fine line.

If you're not careful the 'what ifs' can lead to analysis paralysis where you simply end up spinning and spinning around the debate with no resolution. Well-meaning people unwittingly get locked into a negative mindset where they end up looking more for problems than solutions, and the day is lost. To avoid this, concentrate on the simplest, fastest happy path. During agile planning, in each iteration there will be plenty of time and scope to address the 'what if' scenarios and the not-so-happy paths. We'll cover this in the Do section. For now, your objective is to produce an agreed list of outputs and the stories needed to deliver those outputs as easily as possible for your actors.

One caveat here, however, is to make sure that you do capture the elephants in the room. You definitely want to highlight potential issues and ensure that they're captured and documented. Just don't try and solve them right now. There's an old saying: 'Sleep on it. Things will look better in the morning.' Personally, I've always believed that to be true, and modern cognitive research has verified this. When we hold a challenge in our consciousness, our pre-frontal cortex has limited resources to process it. When the challenge is handed over to our subconscious, a wealth of mental abilities and resources are available to process and generate solutions and ideas. This is the basis of most 'Ah-ha!' moments. It's not that you just had a brainwave in the shower but rather that you've been processing the challenge at a below-conscious level for some time, and when a suitable solution is generated it's passed to the pre-frontal cortex for your awareness.

There's another reason to make sure that all issues raised are captured: Often team members just want to be heard, be recognised and have their issues and objections appreciated. If you try to ignore them as simply naysayers then they'll be naturally resistant to any new ideas and to change. Appreciate their views, acknowledge them, and they'll be so much more willing to work with you than against you.

Wrap up with an ecology check

At this point you're done the main part of the workshop, although there's one final important piece to be covered. Give everyone a ten minute comfort break and get away from the wipe board. Take a quick walk, grab a coffee, check email, call your partner or a friend, do anything that shifts your mindset away from the work.

Then regroup and ask the following questions of the solution as a whole:

- Can we easily integrate this solution into our existing business? The solution has to stand alone and be easy to implement. If the solution relies on a major re-organisation, it's unlikely to fly. Re-think any areas of contention.

- What disruption to existing processes, policies, hierarchies etc might we cause? It's likely that any new proposed system could introduce some disruption to the business. That may well be a good thing and exactly what you're trying to do (eg, replacing outdated, historical, non-viable work practices). Equally, the solution may well cause unwanted disruption in other parts of the organisation. The main point here is to communicate clearly with all parties in order to limit or even negate any unwanted disruption. Explain what you're doing and why, then work though any potential issues. Add these points to your 'elephants' list so that they're captured.

Workshop sample timeline

Below is a list of workshop activities with a guide to the amount of time that should be dedicated to each task. Using this format, an MVP map work-shop can be completed in under five hours, which is very achievable in a single day. Obviously, feel free to tweak the times to best suit your own particular project.

- Set the objective – 10 mins

- Collectively list the actors – 10 mins

- Collectively list the outputs – 20 mins

- Work individually on the 'how' – 30 mins

- Break – 10 mins

- Share and individually review the outputs – 20 mins

- Voting on the best ideas – 10 mins

- Collectively gather the top ideas – 20 mins

- Break – 10 mins

- Iterate through to an agreed solution – limit to 2 hours
- Ecology check – 20 mins

Update your MVP map

Now you're in a position to complete your MVP map. Update your map's actors, outputs and stories. As an example, Figure 2.2 shows part of the MVP map that was produced from a one day workshop at the Met Police during the initial MVP planning for their prosecution application.

How to measure your MVP

Assuming that you've done your homework on your MVPS and added your 'Evidential' SERVE parameter, you'll have clearly identified your marker for successfully completing the project. Additionally, however, there's an opportunity here to identify finer-grained details in the form of traditional KPIs and add them to your stories in your MVP map.

We're probably all aware of the familiar maxim, 'What gets measured gets done', and I for one am a true believer in its power and validity. However, what gets measured and how it gets measured are of paramount importance because if you can't measure what's genuinely important you tend to make what

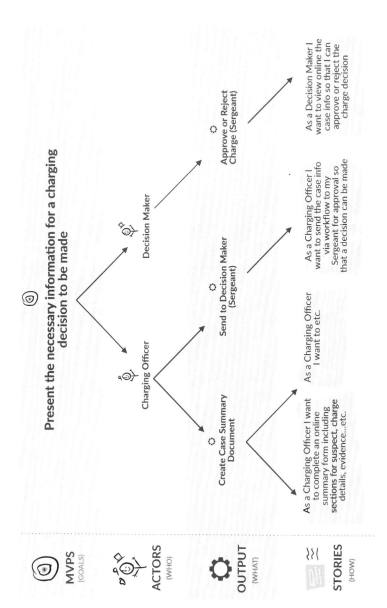

Present the necessary information for a charging decision to be made

MVPS (GOALS)

ACTORS (WHO)

Charging Officer

Decision Maker

OUTPUT (WHAT)

Create Case Summary Document

Send to Decision Maker (Sergeant)

Approve or Reject Charge (Sergeant)

STORIES (HOW)

As a Charging Officer I want to complete an online summary form including sections for suspect, charge details, evidence...etc.

As a Charging Officer I want to etc.

As a Charging Officer I want to send the case info via workflow to my Sergeant for approval so that a decision can be made

As a Decision Maker I want to view online the case info so that I can approve or reject the charge decision

Figure 2.2: MVP Map Structure – completed example

you *can* measure seem important. Take some time out, therefore, to think carefully about specifically what it is that you want to measure and why you're measuring it.

Why would you bother with this extra work if you already have a clear indicator of business success? Well, it's often very useful to measure some KPIs on stories, especially stories related to particular outputs, because you then have an opportunity to review what particular stories had the biggest impact on the delivered business value. Consequently, in a subsequent delivery you can put more effort into those areas with the expectation that they would get you the biggest bang for your buck, as the saying goes.

If you do decide to add some KPIs to your MVP map, then here are some guidelines around measurements to ensure that you capture meaningful data:

- **What will you measure – the scale:** 'The scale' refers to what is being specifically measured. Your business value directive may be to increase new users, increase the number of business 'transactions', increase sales, reduce processing time, etc.

- **How will you measure – the meter:** 'The meter' refers to what unit of measure you want to capture. If you're trying to increase new users, is that a hard number or a percentage increase of existing users? If you're reducing processing times, is that a unit of time or number per day.

- **What's your current situation – the benchmark:** If you're aiming to improve on an existing metric then it's important to know what the current situation is. How many users do you have today? How long does it take to process an order today?

- **What's your minimum Return on Investment (ROI) – the break-even point:** In order for your project to be considered a reasonable success and the resources invested to have been worthwhile, what's the minimum break-even point? What's the minimum number of new users you would expect to generate, for example?

- **What's your target – the real goal:** Here's your opportunity to reach for the stars; but, at the same time, don't set the team up for failure here by setting a totally unachievable target. That will simply demoralise the team rather than energising them to go the extra mile to achieve great success.

Once you've added your KPIs to the individual stories on your MVP map, the map is now fully complete and can be shared with the wider business for review and agreement.

Summary

In this chapter we took our carefully constructed MVPS and built an MVP map. We discussed why MVP maps are important and the information they can convey on a single page. MVP maps detail the actors, outputs and stories that are required to deliver the MVPS. Essentially we detailed the who, the what and the how of your proposed solution.

In this chapter you've also learned how to facilitate an MVP mapping workshop, the logistics required, and you have a clear, timed structure to follow in order to run your own workshop to produce an MVP map. Finally, we looked at potentially adding some KPIs to your map stories, should you decide to do so.

In the final chapter of the Think section we're going to take a look at agile sprint schedules as an alternative to traditional PRINCE2 or waterfall-style project plans. We'll take the output stories from the MVP map to construct a viable sprint schedule that can be delivered in 90 days.

THREE

Sprint Schedule

'If a man knows not to which port he sails, no wind is favourable.'

— Lucius Annaeus Seneca

It's at this point in a traditional project that someone in a project-manager-type role would start to collate estimates for the various tasks required, open up their project plan software of choice and start to draft the ultimate 'project plan' for guaranteed success. As you can probably tell by my sarcasm, I'm not a huge fan of that traditional approach.

Whilst I appreciate that the project plan has been a central component of business management since the 1950s, has no doubt featured in millions of projects and is ubiquitous worldwide, I suspect that today we need something more suited to our modern fast-paced, agile delivery methodology.

In this chapter, I will explain why I believe project plans to be sub-optimal at best, how they lead to longer delivery times, focus the team's attention on the wrong thing and essentially just get on everyone's nerves. Well, mine at least. I'll introduce you to a much more efficient and simpler sprint schedule which focuses the team's attention on what needs to be done, in the shortest possible time, and actually energises the team for success. We'll ditch the linear Gantt-chart approach and delve into timeboxing as a great way to focus on project scope, prioritisation and a fixed delivery date.

Why project plans can be sub-optimal (at best)

A project manager comes to you and says, 'Can you estimate this task for me please as I need to document it on the project plan and work out where it is on the critical path?' That's a perfectly reasonable request, and as a responsible team member you're happy to comply. But what goes through your mind when you hear it?

Firstly, let's review what 'estimate' actually means. An estimate is simply a guess. You're being asked to guess how long a new, unique task is going to take (because every new task is unique). Now, you may have a similar experience to base your guess on, and in some cases it may well be a reasonably accurate guess. But it's still only a guess of what might happen in the future. And who's particularly confident about predicting the future with good accuracy? (Incidentally, if you are one of these rare people please email me next week's lottery numbers.)

So what do you do? You do what anyone in the same position does: you think back to a similar piece of work you've done before and try to remember how long it took. And you add some fat. 'It took a day, so I'll say it took three days just in case I run into any unexpected issues or in case this new task is vastly different from what I expect.'

Now, there's something very insidious about project plans and tasks. A project manager will quite reasonably take your guesstimate and add it to the project plan. In fairness, that's largely all they can do. All of a sudden, though, it's no longer a best guesstimate but a 'contract'. You're obliged and committed to getting that piece of work done in the time you quoted because it says so on the hallowed project plan. I strongly believe that one of the cornerstones of a successful team is personal accountability, so it's quite right that you should commit to doing the piece of work in the time you quoted.

And how many times in the past have you been chastised for work tasks taking longer that you expected or guesstimated? With that hard-earned experience, what do you do? You simply add more fat to cover yourself. So one day's effort of work now becomes a week. You're happy because you're totally confident you can complete the work in a week, and the project manager has a fixed estimate they can put on their project plan. Everyone's happy…

… Except that everyone does the same thing, so the project plan becomes ridiculously long and bears no resemblance to reality. A three- to four-month project is now nine months long according to the project plan. But that's not the worst of it. You know that you've got a week to do what you think is a day's work, so there's no need to rush and get it done now. You can finish off that other piece of work you've still got hanging around or the task you promised the boss you'd get round to so that you can look good. I mean, seriously, who actually does their homework the very day they get it? Who doesn't leave it 'til later? It'll get done, right?

With the deadline approaching, you actually get round to doing the work. Sometimes it only takes a day, as you expected. If so, great. Many times, however, there are some major issues, you don't have access to resources you were counting on, and now you're exceeding your five days. Assuming that you and several other colleagues are now late with work undertaken for the project, subsequent tasks have to be re-scheduled, the Gantt chart needs correcting with new dates and the project end date extends further into the future. At the weekly review, the project manager publishes the new delivery date and marks the project's RAG (red, amber, green) status as 'red', all hell breaks loose and everyone's under pressure. It's not a good place to be.

Aristotle wrote that 'Nature abhors a vacuum', and I suspect the same thing applies to work. If a task is guesstimated as five days' work, guess what? It will take five days. Not because people are lazy – they may actually do the work in one or two days – but they'll naturally keep refining it, polishing it and making it 'perfect' in the five days they have even though 'perfect' is not what we're after. We need team members to get it done and move on.

As if this isn't bad enough, the real issue with project plans is the focus and attention they consume. In reality, a project plan is simply a guess of what might happen in the future, and as such it should be viewed simply as a guide. It has the same scientific validity as the horoscope in your local newspaper. Yes, you can quite rightly argue that it's based on guesstimates of previous work and may therefore be a reasonably accurate model, but it's still a guess, and is that really the best we can do – guess what might happen? There should be too much at stake in your project to guess.

Rather than being perceived as a model, a project plan is commonly perceived more as a bible. Huge amounts of time and effort go into keeping the project plan up to date, correcting dates, dependencies, resources and other details. Management review meetings and decisions revolve around the contents and latest projections of the project plan. Treated this way, it's not a valuable business tool, as originally envisioned by Gantt and others, but simply a log book. The only way you can truly write an accurate project plan log book is to write it the day *after* you complete the project. Is that really useful?

Everyone's focus and attention should be solely on delivery and not updating the project plan; consequently, we need a compelling new tool that discourages team members from protecting themselves by adding fat, focuses attention on product delivery rather than box-ticking project tasks, empowers team accountability and energises the team to get stuff done.

Timeboxing

Before we delve into the mechanics of a sprint schedule it's important at this point to review one of the cornerstones of the Think, Do, Show method (and agile development itself): timeboxing. With traditional project plan methodologies estimates are simply cumulative, and so the end date is no more than the sum of all the parts. Wherever possible, tasks are made parallel rather than sequential so they can be carried out simultaneously, but ultimately the end date is governed by the gathered estimates. And we've seen the kinds of issues that can cause.

When we timebox, on the other hand, we simply allocate a fixed time period (ie, a sprint) and a specific goal for each sprint that advances us towards our MVPS. Then we prioritise the minimum stories that must be in place in order to deliver on the sprint goal.

I have found timeboxing, combined with a clear sprint goal, to be hugely beneficial in every team I've managed, around the world, for several reasons. Firstly, it creates a laser-like focus of the team's attention on the specific requirement for the sprint. There's no dispute about what the team should or shouldn't be doing; it's transparently clear to everyone. Consequently, any noise that comes into the team during the sprint is clearly identified and immediately dealt with.

Secondly, it sets a very clear means of prioritisation for the team. Is this particular story or requirement essential in order for us to deliver on the stated sprint goal, and can it be done in the timebox we have? If yes, then it's high on the priority stack; if not, then it drops down.

Thirdly, timeboxing forces scope limits on stories that are deemed priorities and need to be completed.

Always be asking yourself: 'What's the minimum we can deliver in order to be successful?' This avoids the pursuit of perfection and the constant 'just one more tweak' mentality that consumes so many precious resources without the team realising it.

Lastly, for me personally the most compelling arguments in favour of timeboxing relate to team motivation and wider communication with the business. These will be dealt with in more detail in the Do and Show sections, but for now I'll highlight the key points as they refer to timeboxing and a clearly stated sprint goal:

1. As humans we're wired to complete things. Have you ever noticed whilst drawing on a wipe board during a workshop that, should you not complete an image (three quarters of a circle, for example), someone will pick up the pen and finish the circle? Comedians and storytellers use the same technique. They 'nest' their jokes and stories inside each other so that you're compelled to know the conclusion of every joke, story or anecdote. Even as you're listening to the start of the next story, your subconscious is constantly seeking the conclusion to the previous one. The same thing happens with a timeboxed sprint goal. The team is psychologically compelled to complete it. Individual members of the team feel personal failure if they don't close out the sprint goal. Their subconscious is telling them

something is missing. There is one caveat to this, though: the team has to believe both that the sprint goal is achievable and that they have the skills and resources to complete it.

2. Timeboxed sprint goals force team accountability. Each team member has their own responsibilities to deliver if the team as a whole is to be successful, and there's often nothing more persuasive than peer pressure. No one wants to let the side down.

3. Timeboxed sprint goals can be hugely rewarding. If you're working on a twelve- or eighteen-month-long project, the end goal just seems so far away. It can be difficult to motivate yourself after a few months because the goal never seems obtainable. But if your timeboxed sprint is, say, two weeks long, then it becomes very real. Weight-loss programmes use the same philosophy. Rather than thinking of a year-long programme to lose thirty plus pounds, they continually drive the message of losing just half a pound to a pound this week. Our brains can process and accept that much more easily. As each sprint goal is successfully achieved, this in turn reinforces the motivation to achieve the next sprint, and the next, until finally the MVP is delivered.

We'll talk more about demos in the Show section, but it's worth touching on them here when talking about the motivation for timeboxed sprint goals. Demos are incredibly powerful for two main reasons. Firstly, they give the team a showcase for their hard work in front of their stakeholders, so they get instant feedback and appreciation. In turn, this makes the team feel that they're making rapid progress – because they are.

Secondly, demos build a powerful bond between the delivery team and the business stakeholders. Reading a bi-weekly report on the progress of the project with various charts, RAG status and other elements is one thing, but actually seeing working code in front of your eyes and being able to play with the software is something very different. It's tangible, it's real, and so stakeholders feel far more confident in the ability and progress of the team, leading to greater trust between the two parties, which in turn motivates the team to punch out the next timeboxed sprint goal. Conversely, should things not be going as expected the team has timely feedback and an opportunity to turn the situation around very quickly. It's a virtuous circle for everyone.

Addressing objections

There are a couple of objections to timeboxing that come up often which I'd like to address quickly here. One objection I've often heard is that due to the time limitation scope is often restricted and the delivery team can do a 'rush job'. Under no circumstances should quality ever be affected in a timebox, and we'll discuss guarding against this in detail in the Do section. As for the scope limitation point, my answer would be: 'Good!' We need to deliver just enough of a story to ensure that we can meet the sprint goal and that we deliver the business value. Anything else is nice to have at best or over-gilding the lily at worst. We want that enforced restriction.

The other objection I often hear is that timeboxing is fine for smaller projects but not for larger strategic projects – the argument being that larger, organisation-wide, strategic programmes require far more longer-term planning. This I would totally refute; in fact, strategic programmes require more timeboxing. Yes, they do need a longer-term vision and a longer-term business value delivery, but if you don't timebox them from the start they can very rapidly consume huge amounts of organisational time, money and resources.

If you're reading this book then I assume you have experience of company-wide strategic IT programmes with the vision to revolutionise your organisation's structure and deliver company growth for years to come. How many actually achieve that? I'd guess very few. That's certainly been my experience. If your organisation can pair strategic IT programmes with a timeboxed approach then it really does have the ability to change its future for the better.

Now that we have a good understanding and appreciation of timeboxing, let's look at the mechanics of creating a sprint schedule based on timeboxed sprint goals.

Introducing sprint schedules

By now it should be evident to you that each part of the Think section builds on the previous section. An MVPS forms the basis of an MVP map, and now an MVP map will form the basis of a sprint schedule. We consistently build a joined-up story and set of valuable assets. These assets will be used again as the central communication tool to the wider organisation (this will be covered in more detail in the Show section). This is an incredibly simple, consistent and powerful model. So what exactly is a sprint schedule, and how do you create one?

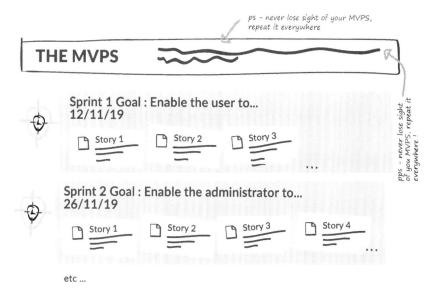

Figure 3.1: Sprint Schedule Template

Let's walk through the components of this sprint schedule template. At the top, reiterate your MVPS so that everyone still knows what they're doing and why. The left-hand column lists the sprint numbers along with their dates. The right-hand column has the sprint goal defined and then lists the stories from your MVP map that will ensure that the sprint goal is delivered.

The sprint goal is the key element here. You can think of sprint goals as milestones if you like – that's what they are from a traditional project management perspective. How, then, do you define the sprint goals and which stories belong to which sprint?

The ninety-day MVP

Collectively (both the delivery team and the business/stakeholders), take a look at your MVP map and logically break it down into sprints. Whenever I work with teams I always use the format of six lots of two-week sprints, which is roughly equivalent to ninety days or a calendar quarter. I can't offer any scientific reasoning or justification for this ninety day project length; in my experience it simply works well as an amount of time to invest in an MVP or an initial phase of a product or delivery. You'll know within this time frame if the envisioned business value is going to be delivered or not.

We're all risk-averse and feel loss far more than we appreciate gain. Organisations, being collections of people, are just the same. For most organisations it's vastly less risky to invest in an initial ninety-day MVP than the huge costs and resources consumed in a traditional long-term project. Organisations can also learn so much about their ability to deliver on a particular product, the technical competence of their people in a potential new area and test market assumptions made within a ninety-day period. It's a sound investment which leads to informed answers to bigger company and market questions that will arise. However, if you feel that your MVP is going to take more or fewer sprints then feel free to adjust it to your own specific needs and the project at hand. Ninety days is a guide, not a defining rule.

Chunking stories

Let's talk more about the chunking element of this exercise. Logically group the chunks of stories that have a start and finish point in isolation of each other. Think about which stories naturally fit together in order to produce one of the outputs on the MVP map or at least get the actor closer to being able to produce the output.

Chunk the stories as best you can. Don't expect the grouping to be 100% perfect – it won't be and that's OK. This is a schedule and not a detailed project plan. Schedules change, and that's fine. Just make sure that the sprints are reasonably challenging for the team without being unachievable.

Build demos into your sprint schedule

Notice that the sprint goal statement starts with 'We will demo…'. Why do you think that is? We've mentioned before the importance of the sprint demo – it's the one opportunity to clearly demonstrate to stakeholders that you've made real progress and are on track. Consequently, when you think about a sprint goal you should think about what it is you're going to demo to your stakeholder. How are you going to prove that you've delivered on your sprint goal? What will you show the stakeholders as clear evidence of success?

After one or two sprints you may find there's a better order in which to address the stories, given what you will have learned about the product, the potential users and the technologies you're using. In which case, adjust the sprint schedule accordingly, make sure you agree the new schedule with the stakeholders, and then re-publish it. When stakeholders see you physically demo progress they'll be far less likely to question your changes as you would have built up their trust. This is a good thing.

Summary

In this chapter we took a look at some disadvantages of traditional project plans and how they can be suboptimal for our purposes, can potentially lead to longer delivery times and can focus the team's attention on the wrong thing. We examined the advantages of a timeboxed approach to projects and then introduced the simpler, yet effective, sprint schedule with clear sprint goals.

As we come to the end of this initial Show section of the book, you now have three key artefacts. These artefacts define the purpose and outcome of your product or project, map out deliverables as to how it will be delivered, and provide a schedule defining the time frame and order of the work involved. It's important to now publish these within the wider organisation and seek approval so that everyone is informed and fully aware of what's going to be done and when. You'll be reusing these artefacts regularly to communicate progress to the stakeholders.

Before we start getting our hands dirty executing our project in the Do section, the final Think chapter is on generating winning proposals. You may well have agreed funding for your product or project already; if not, then you can use the artefacts you have now created to generate winning proposals to both existing organisations and to venture capitalist organisations. In the next chapter, I'll show you how to create such proposals and generate the approval and funding you need to be successful.

FOUR

Creating Winning Proposals

'One should always play fairly when one has the winning cards.'

— Oscar Wilde

In this chapter, I'll show you how you can use the valuable assets you've created in the Think section of the book to present winning proposals to decision makers and stakeholders. Personally, I've always found formal business plans far too dull and abstract. How many business plans and proposals that you've read have left you thinking, 'Wow, I really want to be part of this'? Not many, I would suspect.

Obviously, there's some crucial, and potentially boring, number crunching that has to be part of any business plan or proposal. If the math doesn't add

up and there's no reasonable ROI, then it's very difficult to argue for support and necessary funding. That
makes perfect business sense. Having said that, I do
feel that we can make compelling winning proposals
which energise and motivate stakeholders and decision makers. We'll take a look at what makes a proposal successful and what key factors stakeholders
will look for and expect to be included, along with a
simple proposal template that you can copy and tailor
to your specific needs.

Key elements of a winning proposal

In the eyes of key stakeholders and decision makers,
for a proposal to be truly compelling it needs to con-
tain the following key elements:

- **There's a 'so what?'** – Whatever product, service or
  improvement you propose must fulfil a genuine
  need in order to deliver real business value. If
  you're capitalising on a new business opportunity,
  then you must clearly demonstrate that the
  opportunity exists and quantify it as best as you
  can. Ask yourself what evidence is there to back
  up your claim and use this in your proposal.
  If you're trying to 'scratch an itch' people may
  have, then you must clearly identify those people,
  ideally from amongst the decision makers you're
  presenting to. A friend of mine and former client
  at a major investment bank, Colin Constable,

would ask me whenever I presented to him: 'Simon… what's the *so what* here, for me?' That question always made me think hard about why he should care. I might think my idea is a great one that needs support, but I don't get to make that decision – he does.

- **There's a clear, imaginable user journey –** Stakeholders need to be convinced that the proposal can deliver the proposed business benefit. How will people use the product, and how does the product work? Can stakeholders imagine users loving the product or system and buy into it? Why is it so much better than the status quo?

- **It can be achieved –** Can you show a clear path to successful delivery? What has to happen when, who has to do what, etc, in order to put the product out into the real world for people to use and benefit from?

- **It must have a clear ROI –** No business can be expected to invest in a new product or service unless there's a clear ROI. You need to clearly show these numbers, they need to be valid and you need evidence to back them up. There are some projects that don't have an obvious ROI, such as infrastructure projects; however, these are enablers for other products and services, so if your project falls under this category then identify and accentuate this need.

Given what you've read so far in the Think section, does any of this seem familiar to you? It should do. The 'so what' is very much your MVPS, the 'clear imaginable journey' is the MVP map, the 'it can be achieved' is your sprint schedule, and the 'ROI' is contained in both the MVPS and any KPIs you add to the MVP map.

Assuming you've done your homework, then, you already have the components of a compelling proposal. You simply need to package them into a logical presentation and present it to your decision makers and stakeholders.

Proposal template

1. **Background to the business issue or opportunity –** What specific business problem are you trying to solve, or what opportunity are you trying to capitalise on? Why is it such an important issue or opportunity, and why should your stakeholders and decision makers care?

2. **What happens if you do nothing –** This is an often-overlooked question, but if thought through carefully it can provide a compelling argument to support your proposal. Will you lose market share, revenues, users, customers, etc? Will your competitors strike first and lock you out of any potential future market? Will the continuation of current transactions costs in your business affect

your bottom line? Remember, as humans we fear loss far greater than we appreciate gain. Paint a bleak, but true and reasonable, picture.

3. **What specifically will you fix** – This is simply a reiteration of your MVPS created using our SERVE acronym. If you've successfully identified the business issue or risk and explained what happens if the business does nothing, then a good MVPS can be like an 'Ah-ha!' moment in your audience. They'll feel compelled to hear more.

4. **How will you fix it** – This is where you would present your MVP map. Try to ensure it's as visually compelling as it can be. An MVP map is a brilliant way to show on a single page how the end-to-end solution will look and work. If you have access to graphic designers, then by all means enlist their support in knocking up some simple UI (user interface) screens. Just don't overdo it. You want your audience to believe that it can be a tangible 'thing' with a look and feel, but you don't want to raise lots of usability questions. Less is always more in this instance. One last thing to note here: Do not show the version of an MVP map that includes the KPIs; we'll use that later.

5. **When will you fix it** – Present your sprint schedule along with the specific sprint goals. Stakeholders and decision makers love milestones, and that's exactly what sprint goals are. The schedule also gives a clear timeline to delivery using a

timeboxed approach, which is comforting to stakeholders from a budgetary perspective. They know what the investment is going to be.

6. **Credibility** – Although not always possible or applicable, referencing any previous successes from either members of the proposed team or the business in any related area can be hugely beneficial. Perhaps you're reusing some technology or platform that was successfully used in another project. Maybe some team members have vital domain knowledge and have successfully implemented a similar solution elsewhere. Highlight these as key differentials to success.

7. **Costs** – One of the great aspects of a timeboxed project is that costs are largely fixed; stakeholders love that, it's seems to be a huge comfort blanket for them. Simply make a list of the team members required to deliver the project, use this to cost each sprint and then project the required sprints. Add any additional costs, like hardware, and you're done. Remember, initially you're creating an MVP to deliver a set business value that you've identified. If you're successful then you can talk about an MVP 2.0 and future enhancements.

8. **Return on Investment** – Use a combination of your MVPS and the MVP map with KPIs included to justify your ROI. Simple maths, really – make it as compelling but as truthful and as realistic as you can.

9. **Call to Action** – I see so many great proposals fail because the presenter didn't tell the audience exactly what they wanted them to do next. When the audience leaves your presentation, what specifically do you want to have happen? If you want approval and funding, then ask for it now. If that's not possible on the spot, then set a date for a review and final decision. If the proposal has to go before another board for approval, then task someone with getting you a slot on that board.

Imagine for a moment that you're a decision maker who's been asked to attend a proposal presentation. You know you're going to see a load of slides filled with unfathomable data, the presenter will go on for what seems like hours, there's no clear logic or pattern to what they're saying, and eventually they ask for lots of funding for a project you have little faith in and can't even understand.

Now imagine that this time the presenter highlights a significant issue that exists in your business, and you totally feel the pain and are all too aware of the larger looming issues that arise if this problem is not solved for your business. They then present a concisely worded, feasible solution, with a clear deadline and specific delivery within a fixed time frame. The presenter can demonstrate credibility of previous delivery and has costed the project with a demonstrable ROI. The presenter then asks for a decision. What do you suspect the outcome will be this time?

Summary

In this chapter we took a look at using the assets created in the Think section to create concise, winning proposals. You now have a straightforward, powerful proposal format which can be used to create winning proposals and support for your project. Even if you already have agreed funding, I would urge you to spend a little time creating a simple slide deck of your proposal. Throughout your project you will be asked about it by various people, either those new to the business or senior executives from other parts of your organisations who have heard of what you're doing but don't know the details. This slide deck is a valuable asset that you can use to communicate your message and garner wider company support. Everyone wants to be part of the success, so capitalise on it.

This wraps up the Think section of the book. We've covered a lot of ground and now have a blueprint of what, when and how for software development projects. All we need to do now is execute on the delivery and communicate progress to the organisation and stakeholders.

FIVE

Setting Up Your Organisation's Structure For Success

'Real artists ship.'

— Steve Jobs

The fallacy of the great idea

Everyone seems to be chasing the next big idea, the next big thing, the next global trend. But I strongly suspect that they're missing the key point here. Some years ago, as internet businesses were rapidly replacing traditional bricks-and-mortar stores and online companies like Amazon were on their meteoric rise, it occurred to me that delivery would be the one bottleneck issue that every internet company would face. It's all very well being able to supply the same product at a far cheaper price than traditional businesses, but you still have to physically deliver it.

If customers can't go to your store (because you don't have one), you have to get your product to them somehow. It also occurred to me that the traditional huge logistics delivery firms that would be used by the Amazons of this world had an out-of-date business model, and they could suffer from disruptive internet technologies just as bricks-and-mortar companies could. When you think about it, if as individuals we're not going to the shops anymore, and instead the shops are coming to us, then that creates a lot of logistics to handle and huge potential business opportunity. I also didn't believe that online companies wanted to invest heavily in big logistics operations that weren't part of their key business. I presumed they'd much prefer to use a third-party supplier.

MY BRILLIANT IDEA

I realised that an individual with a car or a van could become their own courier. Using the internet and software apps delivered to GPS-enabled mobile devices like smart phones, I could create an online hub to connect 'suppliers' (ie, individual couriers) to 'customers' (ie, companies that had items to be delivered to individuals).

I thought I could create a Skype-type peer-to-peer business model whereby parties came together to solve each other's business problems. Online companies needed to deliver their goods and individuals needed independent work. It also occurred to me that I'd be releasing a massive latent and flexible labour pool of individuals who could work as and when they wanted to, around their own lifestyles and families.

I ran the idea past everyone I knew and respected in the dot-com world, and they all agreed that it was a fantastic idea and an awesome business opportunity. Everyone I spoke to was instantly energised by the idea and added their own thoughts and value to the discussion. And that's kinda where it ended up – a great conversation piece amongst tech-savvy friends and colleagues over a beer because I never executed on any of it. I didn't know how then.

Around the same time, two other guys had a very similar idea, although their business model involved transporting individuals (ie, passengers) rather than goods. Their company did something I didn't: they executed on their idea. They built a team, they engaged with business and customers, they planned and executed in iterations to build working software, and – most importantly – they shipped. The company they founded is called Uber.

The next big thing isn't just the next big idea, it's the next big idea that's executed upon, brought into the world and gives value to its users. Real artists ship.

These are the key questions we'll address in the Do section of this book: How do you organise your company's resources for optimum delivery, and why do so many companies get it wrong from the outset? How do you build individual crusading teams, then motivate and energise them to turn up each day and do amazing work? Rather than 'engage with your business', how do you create and leverage the power of tribes? How do you plan effective agile iterations, ensuring that the stories you deliver in code are solving real business problems, and ship working code that people genuinely love to use?

I believe there's only one true measurement of success: Shipped software. Software put into the hands of users, where the business value envisioned is actually realised and the investment in time and resources made worthwhile. Also, for a team, I believe there to be nothing more soul destroying than software that sits on the shelf and is never used because it was never finished or shipped to users.

How many millions, if not billions or even trillions, of lines of code are there in the world that never got shipped? How many half-finished corporate projects have you been involved with? So much work gone to waste, so much personal commitment in projects that people truly believed and invested in, but no one even knows about them because they were never shipped. It's quite criminal. But why is that the case? Why is there so much waste, and why do projects fail so often? I suspect that each and every one of us could answer those questions with our own experiences and opinions, some of which would be unique and a lot of which would most definitely resonate with each other.

Ship early, ship fast, build momentum, and take your users and customers with you on the journey – I truly believe that's the key to successful shipping. Sadly, I didn't have this knowledge before, and so my 'brilliant idea' remains just another brilliant idea on the ideas heap. Follow the advice and lessons I've learned over the years, and make sure your brilliant idea is made a reality and you add your value to people's lives. There's no better measure of professional, and personal, success.

Communication across an organisation

TRADITIONAL (SILOED)

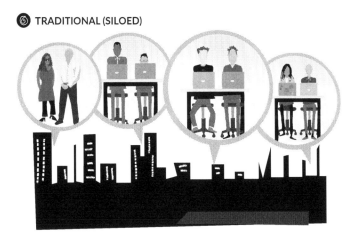

Figure 5.1: Traditional siloed business operations

Virtually all modern-day organisations follow Adam Smith's eighteenth-century theories around the specialisation of the labour force, essentially the breaking down of large jobs into many tiny components. This is true for modern-day knowledge work as much as it is for manufacturing. There are good reasons for that; primarily, it works, and as modern-day work becomes ever more complex it makes sense to have specialists and experts in all fields.

The issue isn't that businesses create silos of operations – that's perfectly natural. The issue is the poor communications, lack of information flow, conflicts between department priorities and department tribalism. Most departments don't even speak the same language. Marketing and product-line people speak one language, business analysts speak another, and developers speak with acronyms and terms that no one understands (except them, of course). True collaboration between these silos is difficult at best and very time consuming.

A few years back we had the 'unified communications' movement. Large corporations like Microsoft, Cisco and Avaya each had their own softwares – IP telephony, video conferencing facilities, etc – that were going to solve these collaboration issues for us. I have good knowledge of unified communications as I worked for BT Plc for a while, as I mentioned in the introduction to this book. Whilst some of these tools are invaluable and we all use some form of them every day, for me they never solved the problem. Collaboration between business operations still remains most companies' biggest issue today. And therein lies the key to successful collaboration.

I believe the closest we've come to date to true collaboration is the agile movement. It focuses a single team on delivering business value, valuing face-to-face communication and discussions, people over process and tools, and working software over documentation. It creates a single team that comes together, learns to speak a single language, and works to create something of value to the world and be part of something bigger than themselves, as individuals or as the skills they possess.

The trouble with water-Scrum-fall

A 2011 Forrester report, authored by Dave West,[11] introduced the world to the agile reality of water-Scrum-fall for most organisations – the reality being that whilst organisations adopt agile development with its close collaboration amongst team members, it's siloed within the development team. That collaboration never seems to exceed the boundaries of the development team. Project Managers still produce complex, over-engineered project plans,

11 Dave West, with Mike Gilpin, Tom Grant and Alissa Anderson, 'Water-Scrum-Fall Is The Reality Of Agile For Most Organizations Today' (July 2011). www.forrester.com/report/WaterScrumF all+Is+The+Reality+Of+Agile+For+Most+Organizations+To day/-/E-RES60109#

business analysts still produce detailed requirement specifications for a product or solution that is embryonic at best. There seems to be this constant need by the business to know the unknowable. All this documentation is then handed over to the development team with a delivery date written down on some guesstimated plan. How, in this environment, is collaboration truly realistic? How is trust ever going to flourish between departments? It's about as futile as standing in a bucket and trying to lift yourself up by the handle. The only way to truly break down barriers between departments is not to have them at all.

⑥ WATERFALL SCRUM FALL

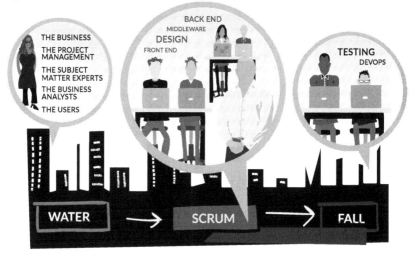

Figure 5.2: Most organisations' water-Scrum-fall model of today

Whilst water-Scrum-fall is a massive improvement and a huge step forward, I believe that, in most organisations at least, the way it and agile in general are implemented suffers from a fundamental flaw. The IT department still has a need to silo its operations to some extent. Back-end services like databases and middleware layers are invariably separated out into various 'platforms'. Whilst I fully appreciate and understand the reasoning behind it, the fundamental flaw for me is that no team can deliver a 'story' (or single piece of business value) on its own, end to end. An application team will need a middleware service from that team to deliver a feature and even support from the database team to store new values not yet modelled in its database.

There's a huge management overhead here in organising and liaising between teams, and that leads to massive waste of resources. Any kind of (inevitable) delay in one area or service has a big domino effect on every other project. Several management meetings lead to project managers desperately starting to re-work their project plans and liaise between projects ineffectively. More time, more delay, more wasted resources. Sound familiar?

I've worked in organisations where the 'platform' teams have asked the application teams what services they think they'll need over the next six months in order that they can be ready in time. What team can possibly answer that question? The application team might have a rough idea, like a login service or an address service, but these are fundamentals which should already be in place. And in order to build a relevant service in readiness, the platform team would need to know the exact data model, what gets passed from the front end to the back and what's expected in return. How is an application team supposed to know that prior to detailed iteration/sprint planning? I can hear some people say, 'Well, they'd have a detailed specification from a technical business analyst to work on'. Have you ever known those detailed technical specifications to remain static, though? Neither have I, which means re-work, more delay, more wasted resources. Again, sound familiar? How, then, can we resolve this issue for good?

Collaboration amongst agile functional teams

The most successful teams I've had the pleasure of collaborating with create teams across the entire business and delivery spectrum. Consequently, every team can deliver a feature and piece of value end to end under its own control. This has a massive positive impact on the team, as we'll discuss later. Firstly, how does this model work?

⑥ AGILE FUNCTIONAL TEAM

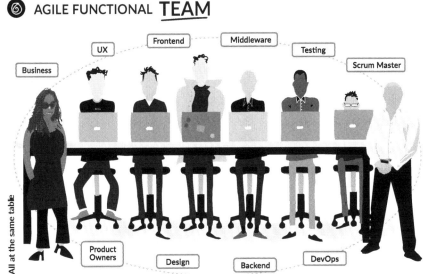

Figure 5.3: Agile functional teams

Functional agile teams are based around a product or specific function, not their department or skill set. They come together as a single entity, with a single vision and identity, regardless of their individual function within the team.

In 2013 I was asked by my friend Rorie Devine to join him at a new start-up in London called Hailo (now acquired by Mercedes and branded under MyTaxi). Rorie was the CTO (chief technology officer) at Hailo and was relentless in his intention to make it a centre of engineering excellence. Rorie not only wanted to build the best software organisation possible, he also wanted all of Hailo to work closely together. I explained my own vision of what that could look like (aka Think, Do, Show), and he wholeheartedly backed me. Rorie's the kind of boss you really want to work for, demanding results but always in your corner.

HAILO

Hailo was a pioneering eHailing application start-up, founded in London and initially providing an eHailing application only to licensed black cabs within London. It's a very different model from that of Uber. Hailo later expanded to several major cities, including Dublin, New York, Tokyo and Barcelona. We organised the teams functionally so that there was one team responsible for the web application that launched and managed cities (setting up zones, zone fees, registering licensed taxi drivers, etc), another team responsible for the driver application which drivers used to accept rides and payment, and a third team responsible for a passenger application that passengers used to eHail taxis and pay.

We made every team autonomous in that, when given a story, they all had the capability and power to envision and design the implementation, write front- and back-end code, and then ship to production. As Uncle Ben told Spiderman, 'With great power comes great responsibility,'[12] so we also made every

---

12 Jonathan Sanford and William Irwin, 'With Great Power Comes Great Culpability', in Philip Tallon, *Spider-Man And Philosophy: The web of inquiry* (May 2012, John Wiley and Sons).

functional agile team accountable for their own work. We told them, 'It's totally your decision to ship, and should it go pear shaped then *you* fix it. There's no fence for you to throw the responsibility over.' That might sound like a poisoned chalice, but the teams embraced it beyond any expectation we had. I never see teams so passionate about quality until you give them this responsibility and accountability. They seem to thrive on it, not back away as one might assume.

The head of product at Hailo at the time, George Berkowski (whom we met in section 1), was able to envision new business value services and hand over to the relevant team. The relevant team would then build a user journey, create a design, write the front- and back-end code, test, demo and, when happy, they'd ship to production then go to the bar to celebrate!

Spotify and Netflix operate using a very similar model and call their teams 'squads'. So there's a music player squad, a desktop experience squad, mobile app squad, etc, each responsible for their product end to end. Not only does this make each team highly specialised in their product but they share a common vision and identity based around that product. They become a passionate tribe, the benefits of which to the company and to the members as individuals are immeasurable. The work defines them and becomes a personal mission. What company wouldn't like to inspire their workforce this way?

One of the concerns this model always seems to raise is that of alleged duplication of work. Whilst teams or squads may be working on different projects they're still part of the same organisation; therefore, duplication of effort must be a factor. One team is surely going to be working on a back-end service which must be similar to another team's service. That is true, but there's an elegant solution that actively encourages reuse of software rather than fostering duplication.

Whilst each team member is assigned to a functional agile team they are also part of a 'guild'. There are guilds for front-end and user experience (UX), business services, database storage – even project and product management. Each guild has a lead who is responsible for promoting reuse where possible and enforcing best engineering or business practice. The guilds meet once per iteration/sprint and discuss what their squad is working on. This fosters amazing collaboration and a deep knowledge between teams of who's working on which features in each functional area. That knowledge share is invaluable to any business. Who actually reads in depth the countless internal communications, slides decks and other documentation that organisations proliferate in an attempt to disseminate this information across the business? Functional agile teams have this knowledge already.

Summary

I started this chapter by explaining that it's the successful implementation of a great idea that most often makes the difference, rather than the brilliance of the idea itself. We then went on to review how setting up a team can have a profound impact on its ability to deliver a successful implementation. Remember, we're talking about the same people here, the same skill sets and so on, just how they're collectively and collaboratively organised. When you think about it, that's a very simple change to make given the huge benefits to be gained.

SIX

How To Build Effective Agile Functional Teams

'Successful organising is based on the recognition that people get organised because they, too, have a vision.'

— Paul Wellstone

In this chapter, I'm going to describe how to set up, manage and motivate functional agile teams. We'll take a look at some of the key roles involved and discuss their main responsibilities. Finally, I'll outline a simple five-step process for creating pep talks that energise and motivate a team to a successful outcome.

Creating functional agile teams

Teams will vary in size depending on the resources available to the organisation. Smaller companies may not have the resources to dedicate skilled individuals to single teams. That's fine as long as the team has direct access to those resources when required – that's a must in order for the model to work in a smaller company.

When forming functional agile teams, there is only one key factor: Teams must be autonomous in that they are able to deliver a story from the back of a napkin to production without having to acquire support from any other teams. Obviously, it's prudent that any organisation implement some kind of quality gating and that the product owner has ultimate decision to release or not. There may be factors outside of the control of the team and even the organisation (such as the introduction of regulatory constraints) that can influence the decision to release to production, but the team must be able to stand alone and deliver the feature itself as well as the business value being delivered.

Key roles of functional agile teams

Product owner

The product owner is responsible primarily for the 'what' – ie, what are you building? They will obviously have a big impact on the MVPS as they're ultimately responsible to the business for the budget spend and ROI. The one key piece of advice I'd like relay here is to do everything you can to have one product owner, and one product owner only, and ensure that they are accessible during the lifecycle of the project. Oftentimes, decisions around the 'what' need to be made quickly, and you need one voice to speak to and provide an immediate answer. Failure to ensure this will delay your project and will cost you dearly in time and resources.

Agile business analyst

A good agile business analyst on a project is invaluable. A traditional business analyst is supposed to act as an interface between the users and the developers. Their role is to speak to users to gather requirements, document them and then liaise with the development team. In my experience, however, the traditional role is less of a facilitator and more of a barrier. I often think of the traditional role as Chinese whispers – the developers get a third-hand interpretation of what the requirements and deliverables are.

A business analyst on an agile functional team is a true facilitator. As they have both technical and business expertise they can supply support across the project. I've used their expertise in agile functional teams to help the business and their users understand the root cause of problems, and to facilitate user-centric workshops and business journey mapping. Conversely,

I've used their technical skills to support the development team too, such as when researching available APIs, evaluating technical specifications and facilitating technical workshops.

Project manager

Traditional PRINCE2, Waterfall-environment project managers assume a lot of responsibility within a project regarding scope, timelines, delivery dates and other elements. In functional agile teams these responsibilities are shared amongst the self-organising and autonomous team members where everyone is accountable. Therefore, project managers aren't necessarily required in that traditional way. Having said that, in large organisations having a project manager assigned to an agile functional team can be useful, resources permitting.

Whilst most organisations may adopt agile practices in their development environments, that's sadly not normally true for their day-to-day business operations. There remain numerous legacy processes and procedures regarding procurement, personnel, contracts, HR and other aspects of the business that a project manager can provide assistance with. There's a lot of 'grunt' work that is required in large organisations. I would always look to keep this grunt work outside the agile functional team as it just slows the boat down. A project manager can greatly assist with this.

Scrum Master

The Scrum Master plays a critical role in a functional agile team. Their main responsibilities are threefold, namely to protect the team, coach the team and communicate to the business.

In order to protect and shield the team, a good Scrum Master will minimise all outside distractions. Development, testing and business analyst resources are precious commodities that need to be protected. It always baffles me when I see organisations hire expensive skilled resources to write code and then drag them into lots of business meetings. Software developers need to be concentrating on writing good-quality code that delivers the MVPS, not sitting in meetings because a business leader has requested their presence. A good Scrum Master should stop this and give the developers space and time to work. Removing these kinds of impediments to delivery is the Scrum Master's responsibility.

Scrum Masters are also responsible for coaching and running the team. I'm a great believer in self-organising teams and allowing the team to dictate how it works, but with full accountability (more on this later). A good Scrum Master will coach the team in agile principles and make sure that the agile rituals such as daily stand-ups, planning sessions, demos and retrospectives take place, rather than merely dictating how the team operates. The focus should always be on how to 'make the boat go faster' and improve team velocity.

Finally, the Scrum Master should be the conduit to the business, sometimes in conjunction with a good business analyst. They should be handling all outside communications with the business and stakeholders, including the one-page report (which I'll introduce in the Show section). Composing the MVP map and the sprint schedule are typical responsibilities, too.

If the Scrum Master runs good demonstrations, composes and distributes a one-page report and communicates effectively with the business, then this will automatically reduce interference from the outside. If the business has confidence in the team and can see real progress at demonstrations, then they'll naturally leave the team alone to get on with delivery. If this is handled poorly, however, then the business will naturally want to micro manage the team and interfere. Consequently, this is a vital responsibility of the Scrum Master which is sometimes overlooked.

Designer/UX

When I first set out in software development I always thought that designers were somewhat of a luxury and there simply to 'put lipstick on the pig'. But then I met and was introduced to the work of Marty Neumeier when he gave a speech at Ribbit in Mountain View, California. (Ribbit was a VoIP start-up that was acquired by BT Plc.[13]) After listening to Marty, and subsequently reading his books, I now hold the polar opposite view. Having good designers and UX people on board can make or break a project. Part of the subtitle of this book – 'building software people love to use' – is my homage to great designers, like my friend Pete who branded this book and did all the artwork.

And it's not just about making software look beautiful but making it functional too. Getting the UX right is vital for any project. Great designers, like Pete, will work closely and iteratively with the users to do what I call 'shortening the journey'. By 'journey' I mean the user journey of how a piece of software actually works for a user. If you can shorten the user journey, you'll save users time and effort, and that's what they'll love about your software. Remember Hailo's 'two taps to a taxi'? If it was ten taps, would people use it? Probably not. The Uber app works in a similar way – you just have to tell it where you're going and it does the rest.

So now, a good designer is one of the first names on the team sheet for any functional agile team that I build or manage.

---

13 'BT Snaps Up Ribbit for $105m' (July 2008). www.telegraph.co.uk/finance/newsbysector/mediatechnologyandtelecoms/2793933/BT-snaps-up-Ribbit-for-105m.html

Developers

The key to good developers in a functional agile team isn't skillset, it's mindset. Of course, developers need the basic skills of code writing, but I want to see a mindset of accountability and responsibility. During planning, the developers collectively agree to deliver whatever stories are being developed in that next sprint, and therefore that becomes their sole responsibility. In functional agile teams the team can dictate how it works, but always with accountability. Netflix has a term for this kind of culture which they call 'freedom and responsibility'. Netflix teams not only dictate how they work but they can also dictate what tools they use, their platforms and other details. Ultimately, though, Netflix teams are held responsible and accountable for their work. It should be said that this kind of culture doesn't suit everyone. Some people like to be told what to do and how to do it. These kind of people don't work well in functional agile teams.

How can you tell if someone will work well under a culture of accountability and responsibility? You ask them this simple question and listen to their response: 'How do you know when you've done a good job?' What you're listening to in their response is either internal or external points of reference. People will invariably say one of two things: Either they just know they've done a good job (internally referenced) or they'll say that someone like their boss or a customer tells them they've done a good job (externally referenced). In my experience, internally referenced people are more suited to a culture of accountability. That's not to say that externally referenced people can't work in this culture, but they will need coaching and support.

Automation tester

No software is ever bug free, especially today as software becomes more complex and the way users interact with it changes. I've seen bug reports where the detailed steps to reproduce the bug go on for pages and pages. No matter how good your testing is, no one would ever think to write a test to guard against such bugs. So what do you do about them?

My advice here is to have a solid automation tester on the team, then ship and fix on demand. People think nothing of updating their phone or computer software as new versions are shipped and bug fixes get introduced. Apple, Microsoft, Google and similar companies ship patch releases and bug fixes every week, and we think that's fine. But inadvertently introduce a bug in our business software and everyone freaks out. Obviously we do everything we can to mitigate it and test thoroughly, but it's gonna happen at some point, so learn to deal with it. Continuous delivery forces us to carry out a great deal of regression testing. A good automation tester can save hours of manual testing time by creating automated scripts to carry out regression testing. Good regression testing also gives the business confidence that nothing has been broken, giving them more confidence to allow you to ship and fix on demand.

DevOps engineers

For some weird reason that I can't understand, DevOps engineers aren't normally part of development teams. They're seen as a separate function to development and are therefore kept in a separate team. Agile functional teams, however, always include the DevOps engineer(s) as part of the development cycle. No matter how well-crafted and beautiful your software is, without DevOps engineers you can't ship. Having them as part of the development cycle makes for faster delivery and shipping too.

Users/subject-matter experts

It's imperative that you bring your users and any subject-matter experts into the development lifecycle. Taking them on the journey with you is vital if you want your software to succeed and be loved. I always allow them to listen in to daily stand-ups, but I ensure that they don't participate. If they have questions then they can approach the Scrum Master after the stand-up, otherwise they would consume precious development time. It's also important that users and subject-matter experts feel listened to and their comments and opinions taken on board. You can't always solve their issues or concerns, but it's important that you listen and then give feedback and suggest potential alternative solutions. It's equally easy to make users your greatest ally or your greatest enemy.

Managing the team

'I hire smart people and get out of their way.'
— Lee Iacocca

In my experience, the best way to manage a team is to not bother. If you hire smart people, give them a vision of what you want and get out of their way, then they'll pretty much manage themselves. I'm also a strong proponent for self-organising teams. No team works in a vacuum inside an organisation, and, therefore, each team has to work within a given framework of set rules; outside of this, however, do everything you can to allow the team to self-organise. A self-organised team feels empowered and trusted by the organisation. They will naturally want to repay that trust by managing themselves appropriately and doing great work. It's the simplest and easiest thing you can do rather than trying to micro manage everyone, which just doesn't work.

GOOGLE'S 'PSYCHOLOGICAL SAFETY'

Google carried out some interesting research recently using its big data tools to discover what its top-performing teams had in common. What Google discovered is surprising and, I suspect, has far reaching ramifications for all organisational teams. They discovered that in their top-performing teams the dynamics between the team members themselves was far more important to success than the skills of the individual members. People in self-organising teams that fostered an attitude of what Google termed 'psychological safety' were far more successful than teams with 'star players' and highly skilled individuals. By 'psychological safety', they refer to a team culture where individuals feel safe to take risks and raise objections or ideas without the fear of being embarrassed.[14] In a self-organising team, that's a natural occurrence.

In his excellent book *Drive*,[15] Daniel H Pink talks about 'motivation 2.0' for the digital era. Gone are the carrot-and-stick forms of motivation, and Pink illustrates how successful teams now want autonomy, mastery and purpose. Self-organising teams are autonomous by default. A good MVPS will equip

14 Julia Rozovzky, 'The Five Keys To A Successful Google Team' (November 2015). https://rework.withgoogle.com/blog/five-keys-to-a-successful-google-team

15 DH Pink *Drive: The surprising truth about what motivates us* (2009). www.danpink.com/books/drive

your teams with a clear purpose and allow them to master their craft and delivery.

Motivating the team

As stated above, the best way to motivate your team is to give them a clear purpose and provide them with a *why* and not a *how*. They should be left to discover the how themselves. That's exactly what a MVPS does, and if the team has been directly involved with creating the MVPS then they all share a clear and undisputed purpose to their work. That's powerful stuff for individuals. Who today can fully articulate what they're doing and why? I suspect not many team members can.

There are a couple of very simple things you can do that have a profound effect on team motivation. Firstly, if you're writing enterprise systems for an internal user group or even a known external user group, take the development team to where the users are. Get the users to show the development team first-hand the business issues that your software will solve for them. This human connection to the user group has a massive impact on the development team. Requirements and features become very personal when the development team see the pain that users face day to day. A story is no longer then just a card on a board but a problem that the development team are solving for a real person whom they've actually met.

Motivating with demonstrations

We'll discuss demonstrations, and how to make them effective, in detail in the Show section of the book. I believe that the majority of the time not enough effort is put into demonstrations. Many agile teams view them a waste of time and a nuisance. However, demonstrations are a perfect motivational tool, if done properly. The Scrum Master needs to take a lead role here, ensuring that stakeholders and users attend and that the required time and effort from the team is devoted to demonstrations.

A good demonstration with instant feedback from real users and stakeholders is a massive shot in the arm for the team. They fire up the team to work on the next iteration, which is why I always recommend holding planning sessions straight after demonstrations. The development team come into planning with a sense of achievement and expectation to do more in the next iteration.

Pep talks

Being able to deliver a good pep talk to a team is an important skill. Some people are natural motivators and seem to have an innate empathy with teams, which enables them to give rousing speeches. For the rest of us, however, there is a simple process that you can follow which will produce magical results in your teams. Also, knowing when to give a pep talk is very important. If you decide to give a pep talk at the start of every iteration then they lose their impact, no matter how well you deliver them. So keep them for crucial points during the project lifecycle such as the start of new phase or a go-live point for a new product.

Pep talk process

Follow this simple five-step process to deliver great pep talks:

Step 1: 'Here's what I'm asking you to do' – List out the specific actions that you want the team to perform. For example, when I'm carrying out a significant deployment of rollout of a new project I will list all the actions that need to take place and also assign specific names to the actions. That way, everyone knows what's expected of them and in what specific orders actions need to be carried out.

Step 2: 'Here's why it's important and why you should care' – Revisit your MVPS here and the specific business value that the team will deliver. If you've been able to connect your development team with real users and their pain, then use that as a motivational driver too: 'Because of the software you're going to deliver, Janet from the back-office team won't have to spend many boring hours each day completing those spreadsheets and can concentrate on helping real customers fix their issues.'

Step 3: 'Here's why I know you can do it' – List out the specific skills the team members have that will enable them to complete the actions. This gives the team confidence that they can achieve what you're asking them to do.

Step 4: 'Think about what you've done together before' – Refer to any previous examples of when the team have achieved success together. Again, this boosts the team's confidence of success.

Step 5: 'Now let's go do it' – Give the team a clear vision of what success is going to be like. Use language that enables them to see, feel and even hear what will be different when they've achieved the goal.

Summary

By now you should be fully aware of the main roles and responsibilities of functional agile team members. We reviewed managing the team and reusing our MVPS as a driver for motivating self-organising teams with purpose and passion. And when a key milestone in the lifecycle of your project arises, you now have a simple five-step process for producing a pep talk to energise the team to success.

SEVEN

The Importance Of Tribes

'I've learned that people will forget what you said, people will forget what you did, but people will never forget how you made them feel.'

— Maya Angelou

What a tribe is and why you need one

In his 2007 book *Tribes*,[16] Seth Godin introduced us to a broader concept of 'tribes'. In this context, tribes are groups of like-minded individuals who share a passion, whether they want to change the world in same way or just love playing a particular video game.

---

16 S Godin, *Tribes: We need you to lead us* (2008, Piatkus Press).

In *Start With Why*,[17] Simon Sinek links the concept of tribes to companies and their products using Apple as a case in point. Apple's marketing very much plays to the audience of their own tribe, who love their products and great design. The earlier marketing campaigns of Mac computers were always headlined with the slogan: 'Think Different'. Tribal members think differently about a product or problem because of their passion. They tend to love a product or service because they're often angry and want to change the world or their industry somehow.

What does this have to do with your project? Since reading Godin and Sinek's books, I've used the concept of tribes to garner passionate support for a project. Whatever your project or audience size, you can do the same.

Both the traditional waterfall model and the water-Scrum-fall model we learned about in Chapter 5 naturally exclude tribe members. After the initial interaction with users to gather requirements, they are often out of the picture until the project is completed or nearing completion for sign-off purposes. Engaging with users and potential tribe members after you've built the product and merely asking them to carry out user acceptance testing is too late. And, quite honestly, at that point in the process why should they care? They were not consulted or involved in the

---

17 S Sinek, *Start With Why: How great leaders inspire everyone to take action* (2011, Penguin).

development process, other than to carry out tick-box sign-off activities. They were never brought into the development team, made part of the iterative process and actively listened too. You can't expect to win their hearts and minds *after* the event.

Tribe members must be engaged from day one of any project and brought in to actively shape the product or solution. This way, they take ownership of the solution and get what they want and need in order to deliver the required business value, rather than being told what they need by someone else who may not know the organisational landscape that they work in so well.

A TRIBE AT THE MET

When my team at the Met Police in London created its commendation-winning prosecution solution, we created a tribe by engaging with officers from day one. The officers we engaged with were an integral part of the team. They innately understood the pain that officers went through every day in creating a prosecution case for the Crown Prosecution Service. The officers became so passionate about the system the team produced that they themselves extended the tribe. During presentations, they used the tag line for the system: 'Built by officers, for officers'. By engaging directly with officers in police stations across London they created tribe members they called SPOCs (Single Points of Contact) in every station. These SPOCs were not appointed but naturally came forward as they were equally passionate about creating a great service for their colleagues. They wanted to make their part of the world better.

In 2018, following a visit to the Met Police by the Assistant Commissioner of the Singapore Police Force (SPF), I was asked to present to the SPF in Singapore regarding digital transformation. During the presentation, I talked about how we ship a major new release every ninety days. I was asked by the Head of Digital Transformation at the SPF how we could possibly train all 30,000 police officers in time every ninety days when we ship new features and functionality. He asked me how many trainers we had and how training was delivered. I told him the answer: we didn't have any trainers because we didn't need them. We had a tribe.

The tribe members – the SPOCs – know all about the new features because they were actively involved in building them. They were involved with planning them and creating the user journey for them, and they knew exactly how each feature worked. Before a major release the SPOCs executed the training in their own police station with their colleagues. They also did any necessary hand holding when a major release came out and fed back any issues officers were facing or bugs that may have come up.

One of the biggest issues with any new system is garnering take-up and getting people to use it. Tribe members accelerate take-up by speaking passionately and extolling the virtues and features of new systems. They know exactly the issues and pain of your intended audience because they come from and are part of that audience. Consequently, they act as great ambassadors and salespeople for your project.

How to create a tribe and keep it engaged

How do you create a tribe? Tribe members aren't selected, they come forward. They come forward themselves because they want to be part of something they're passionate about and change the status quo, which they often hate. Imagine the difference between a tribe member who freely engages because they believe in the project and someone who's been told by their boss that they've got this new responsibility added to their already burdensome workload. The latter is not the kind of tribe member you want; the former sees that they can become part of the development team, that they are listened to and their opinion valued.

Willing volunteers are hard to find, so I would recommend looking for the people that are regarded by their managers as a pain in the ass – the people who complain specifically about the area of your project. Ask them: 'Is this problem important enough for you to want to make a difference?' If they say that they'd like to but don't have time, or their workload precludes them from taking on any other work, then pass them by. But if they say yes, then you've just found yourself a new tribe member.

When you find new tribe members, be honest with them. You're not going to be able to solve all their problems, and sometimes, whether for technical or business reasons, you're not going to deliver everything they want. But that's OK; tell them that they're very much regarded as a key member of the team and that they will be openly and honestly listened to and their opinions will be sought. They can still make a huge difference and shape the future of your project. Being part of something bigger than yourself is what we all crave and aspire to.

It's important that you give tribe members access to the new features before shipping to production. They're keen beta testers, so use that to your advantage. They want to be involved and be able to show colleagues and other users new features. It's great if you have some kind of separate platform for their use, ideally in the cloud somewhere that users have easy access to from any device (Amazon or Azure are services I often use). At the end of each iteration or sprint, ship to that platform so they always have the latest version. It's amazing how much feedback you will get.

With regards to feedback, don't expect it all to be positive. Sometimes tribe members are at odds with one another, and there will be times when decisions have to be made in the interests of the business and project rather than the tribe members. The key point here is to openly acknowledge the feedback and communicate with your tribe. Tell them honestly why decisions were made and, whilst they may not agree, they will respect your integrity and openness.

Summary

I would urge you to consider engaging with a tribe for your project, whether your tribe is two or three people or two or three hundred people. A tribe can really make a project successful and is essentially a 'free' resource. What project wouldn't benefit from passionate advocates who give up their time to promote the amazing work the development team are doing and the business value being realised?

EIGHT

Agile Rituals

'Whatever affects one directly, affects all indirectly.'
— Martin Luther King, Jr.

As I mentioned in the main introduction of this book, this is not a starter's guide to agile. I make the assumption that you already know the basics of agile, including the rituals such as stand-ups, planning, demonstrations and retrospectives.

Whenever I'm asked to consult for companies, the people there always tell me that they're keen agile practitioners. However, when I sit in on their rituals, I experience one-hour stand-ups, all-day planning sessions, almost no demonstrations and a whole manner of other bad practice.

Agile rituals should be focused on brevity, ensuring everyone knows what to do, keeping everyone updated on progress, quickly identifying and dealing with impediments and blockers, and ultimately maximising real work time. That's why we perform them. I've seen some companies 'practicing' agile where the time given to carrying out the rituals is greater than time devoted to actually doing the development work required to deliver the software. It's very easy in a typical two-week sprint to lose upwards of 50% of your development time in rituals and meetings. Consequently, projects take twice as long and cost twice as much to deliver. That's a sobering thought.

Agile rituals need to be contained and controlled in order to maximise their effectiveness and reduce their impact on development time. In this chapter, I'm going to revisit the agile rituals and outline the key dos and don'ts. I'll also introduce some new things you can do that will save you a great deal of time and stress during an iteration or sprint.

Why the agile rituals are so important

The classic agile rituals of stand-ups, planning, demonstrations and retrospectives define the operating framework and day-to-day logistics of running an agile software project. They are, in fact, the way we implement the *Agile Manifesto*[18] and the associated

---

18 Beck et al, *Manifesto*, 'Principles behind the Agile Manifesto'.

agile principles. Sprint demonstrations in particular are one of the most, if not *the* most, important agile rituals. They are so vital that we won't discuss them here as I've dedicated a whole chapter to them in the Show section of this book.

Incidentally, why do we call these practices 'rituals'? Rituals play an important role in society in general. Rituals remind us of what's important in our lives, and they also provide a sense of stability and continuity. You can also use rituals to work more effectively and stay focused on your goals. For me, that's what the agile rituals do too. They provide the team with a consistent operating framework and a daily sense of both stability and continuity in which to work. Each member of the team knows that an iteration (or sprint) is kicked off with planning, everyone knows the stand-up is first thing in the morning (or whenever they decide to hold it), and everyone knows they're working towards a great demonstration at the end of the sprint, followed by a chance to reflect on how the work went during a retrospective session.

I believe that, if carried out properly, agile rituals also bind the team together. This is especially true in autonomous, self-organising teams where members feel free to speak openly. For these kinds of teams, the rituals become a focal point, allowing the team to get together, express themselves freely, share experiences and learn from each other in a way that puts the project and the delivery first, not just having meetings that 'tick boxes' in a non-agile framework.

The rituals also reinforce accountability amongst the team. During the daily stand-up, team members are asked what they achieved the previous day. If a team member repeatedly says 'not much' then it's pretty obvious quite quickly that the team member isn't performing optimally. Perhaps they're struggling with their particular story or a technology framework, for example. Then the Scrum Master and team can intervene at an early stage to better support that team member and get them contributing faster to team success.

Before I delve into best practice for the agile rituals, I want to touch on two points, namely agile boards and sprint length.

Agile boards

Whilst I'm a big fan of agile software like JIRA, VersionOne and Workzone, I'm also a huge proponent for a physical Scrum board, especially for co-located teams. In my own projects I use an electronic tool, such as JIRA, and a physical board with columns titled 'backlog', 'blocked', 'in development', 'in test' and 'done'. At the start of a sprint, I create index cards with the story headline, software reference number (if applicable) and the story points allocated by the team during planning. All of the stories start in the backlog column on the far left at the start of the sprint. Each team member is then asked to put their name on their stories and physically move them from one column to the next as they progress their work. I've found that the best boards are the magnetic ones, simply because it's so much easier using magnets to hold index cards in place and move them around, rather than Blu Tack or Sellotape. I've even had fridge magnets made with the team members' photos on them – a bit over the top, but it was a lot of fun too, with everyone pulling funny faces and certain raised digits!

Now, you could rightly argue that having software tools and a physical board is a duplication of work effort. So why do I think it's so important, and why am I such a proponent of using a physical board? Firstly, it's a great focal point for the team during the daily stand-up. The team gathers around the board, and everyone can see at a glance exactly where the project is and who's working on what. Secondly, everyone can see if a particular story isn't physically moving. Maybe no one's picked it up from the backlog, in which case we would ask why not. Maybe a team member has been working on a story far longer than the story points dictate. Again, we would ask why that might be. This is a great opportunity to offer help and support to potentially struggling team members.

Thirdly, the team can instantly see the progress of work during a sprint. If halfway through the sprint only 10% of stories are done and most are still in the backlog, then it's obvious they have a problem which can be addressed. Fourthly, a physical board is a great visual aid for stakeholders and management to review. Whenever I get an email requesting a report on progress, I simply tell the requester to come and see the board and speak with the team. It might seem impertinent at first, but I've had product owners tell me that one of the highlights of their day is to pop in to look at the Scrum board as they leave for home.

All of the above can, of course, be done with agile software on a large screen, but it never feels the same. Many developers and testers have commented to me that there's something very visceral about physically moving their stories on a hand-written card from one column to the next, especially to the 'done' column. It's extremely satisfying to see your own work progress through the sprint and know that you've contributed to the team's success. You just don't get that same tangible feeling with software tools.

Sprint length

I'm often asked, 'What is the ideal iteration, or sprint, length?' Although I'll often say that there's no ideal length as such, because each project has its own specific dynamics and constraints, I do think that there is a best practice when it comes to sprint length, which I believe is two weeks.

I have worked in weekly sprints before; however, the stories were very much known, understood and repetitive, so very little planning was required. When I worked for a major UK mobile operator, most of the software work was web content detailing the latest contract options. In cases such as that one, if you factor in the overhead of agile rituals such as stand-ups, planning, demonstrations and retrospectives, then weekly sprints for most projects just don't work. You'll spend a large percentage of your potential development time planning and organising the work, rather than actually doing it.

Monthly sprints are just far too long. All things being equal, you'd think that the team velocity for a two-week sprint would double for a monthly sprint. It doesn't; I've tried it a few times as an experiment. In my experience, you get an increase of around 10% to 20% in velocity. There's a kind of Parkinson's Law mindset that creeps in with monthly sprints. Even though we might plan and story point the appropriate velocity, team members think they have more time than they actually do. Work just seems to take longer and longer.

I've found two-week sprints to be the ideal. Ideal because you can allocate sufficient time and carry out the agile rituals well without impacting detrimentally on development time. Ideal because there's enough time to carry out the work – but only just – so the team is kept focused on delivery and execution but not stressed over it or thinking they have more time than they do. And ideal from a stakeholder perspective. Attending a demonstration every two weeks keeps stakeholders engaged and enthusiastic about the project without being burdensome to their already-busy schedules.

Sprint planning

Whether I'm coaching or speaking at a conference, I'm often asked: what is the agile ritual that teams struggle with most frequently? I always answer 'Planning', and the audience always moans and groans in agreement. But the misconception in the audience is that teams don't plan enough, whereas my view is that they plan too much.

When I say they plan too much, what I really mean is that they spend too much time planning. I've often witnessed teams spending a full day planning a two-week sprint. That's ridiculous – it's 10% of your potential development time in one planning meeting. And the thing about meetings is that they often lead to more meetings.

But why is that? Why do teams spend hours doing so-called 'planning'? In my experience, there are two key factors at play here. Firstly, there's been no prior thought about the upcoming sprint and what needs to be achieved. Consequently, planning is like the first day at school when everything is new, everyone's finding their feet, and that process just consumes time.

Secondly, there's no real focus on the sprint delivery, and so the team members are having to context-switch between several different stories with no unifying theme to help them tie stories together. Then they lose concentration and start to get bored. When they're bored they get distracted by anything: playing with their phone, the argument they had with their partner or a friend earlier, the shopping they need to get on the way home. Anything but the task at hand. Because they're not concentrating on what is said, people have to repeat themselves several times. When people are in this mindset it's very hard to think creatively and to be at all productive. Again, this whole situation just consumes time in abundance. No wonder teams can spend a full day 'planning'.

How do we fix this? We break up planning into two easily manageable chunks – pre-planning and planning – which, even when combined, shouldn't take longer than two hours.

Pre-planning

In Chapter 3, I introduced the concept of a sprint schedule and the sprint goal statement, which starts with the phrase, 'We will demo...'. Before you start sprint planning it's important that everyone, including the product owner, the stakeholders and team members, have a big-picture, holistic view of what needs to be delivered in the sprint. Rather than concentrate on disparate, unrelated features, put the team's efforts into delivering a complete and specific part of the user journey from the MVP map. This way, the team is empowered to deliver real business value rather than a shopping list of separate features. To me, this is what the term 'pre-planning' is all about.

Pre-planning does not need to involve the whole team and should take no more than thirty minutes. Required participants include the product owner, Scrum Master or project lead, the business analyst, and one or two software developers. Hold the pre-planning session two or three days prior to the end of the current sprint. The objective is to review the sprint goal statement from the MVP map and ensure that it's still relevant given the development to date and progress of the project. It's then the product owner's responsibility to select the minimum set of stories from the backlog that will deliver the sprint goal which can be demonstrated by the team.

Once the stories have been selected, the Scrum Master or project lead and developers need to ask the product owner some simple questions around the stories. Such questions can include: 'In this story, what happens if a user does x?' or 'In this story, have you thought about y?' or 'How does this story relate to that one?' The product owner and business analyst are not expected to have the answers at hand to these questions. The whole point is that the questions are food for thought.

The product owner and business analyst then go away, spend time thinking about the questions, and review their stories, the user journey and any other relevant information so that they can attend the sprint planning meeting much better equipped and informed. Hence the reason for holding pre-planning two or three days prior to the new sprint – it gives them sleep time to digest the questions and think carefully about the business value being delivered in the sprint goal.

Planning techniques

My advice here is to always hold your planning session straight after a demonstration. After a great demonstration everyone is fired up and ready for the next sprint in a creative, problem-solving, can-do frame of mind. Start the planning session with a vocalisation of the sprint goal from the pre-planning session in the form of 'We will demo the ability to...'. This sets the overall frame of the sprint and gives the team a focal point of delivery. Assuming the product owner and business analyst have adequately prepared following the pre-planning session, planning should merely be an execution of basic agile planning techniques based around the stories required to deliver the sprint goal.

So, what are the basic planning techniques and best practice? Firstly, make sure you have the minimum attendees required: the Scrum Master, developers/software engineers, business analyst (if you have one), testers, the product owner, and perhaps a subject-matter expert (user), should specific story questions arise that the product owner may not be able to answer. That's it, you don't need or want anyone else in attendance.

It's important to understand that an agile planning session is solely an agile team activity, the purpose of which is to establish, as best as possible, which stories will be developed in the next sprint to deliver the sprint goal. It's the agile team who have to commit to delivering the work and are consequently made accountable for the delivery. If you desire a self-organised, empowered, successful team then you have to allow them to plan their work appropriately and take the relevant responsibility. Therefore, you don't need superfluous attendees, who will no doubt ask uninformed, irrelevant questions, even if they are well meaning.

Planning sessions that do not have a clear outcome, where the requisite pre-work has not been carried out, and that are attended by too many people, take all day and achieve very little. Successful planning sessions keep the focus on the sprint goal, are attended only by the people who will actually do the work and have the product owner/users there to answer specific story questions.

Planning poker and story points

I don't know precisely what it is about the concept of story points, but many people struggle with them. Some people just get it, but many don't. I suspect it has something to do with the abstract nature of the concept. As humans we try to understand new things in the context of things we already know. A story point isn't a unit of time, and it isn't a unit of cost or value. So it's hard, as a coach, to relate story points to a known concept. I used to spend hours trying to explain the concept, and I could sometimes see in the faces of those I was explaining it to that I might as well have been speaking an alien language. Then I developed the story point guide I'm going to introduce you to, and everything changed. Now I don't even bother trying to explain the story point concept to team members. I just put up the guide on a screen, explain how it works and then we start playing planning poker.

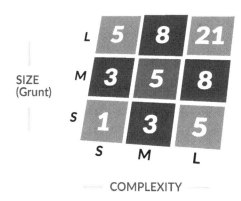

Figure 8.1: Story Point Guide

As you can see from Figure 8.1, the story point guide has a vertical axis relating to 'grunt' in three simple increments of low, medium and high. Then there's a horizontal axis relating to 'complexity', again in increments of low, medium and high. 'Grunt' refers to development effort (ie, Are there a lot of lines of code to write? Is there an existing pattern that could be used, or is it a new block of code work?). 'Complexity' refers to how complicated the feature is (ie, Are we dealing with a complex algorithm? Are we using a new set of APIs we have no prior knowledge of, or are we reusing existing API knowledge?).

Here's the template for using this simple guide to crunch through stories and estimate accurately:

1. The story is quickly read aloud

2. Allow a few minutes for any questions the team may have for the product owner and any users present

3. Each member of the development team assesses the story with regards to both grunt and complexity in terms of the scale, small, medium or large

4. Using the matrix above, each member of the development team selects the number relating to their assessment (eg, medium grunt and medium complexity = 5 story points)

5. Each member of the development team votes on the story using traditional planning poker cards or a smartphone app (I always prefer smartphone apps, simply because they're easier to manage)

6. Should there be differing opinions regarding story size, I prefer to ask the team member with the higher value to justify their decision. The onus is on them to convince the other team members that perhaps there's a complication or a complexity they hadn't thought of. The Scrum Master needs to be wary here that team members aren't just 'covering their backs' and adding extra comfort time. In a truly empowered, self-organising team this is less of an issue as their intent is to deliver as much value as possible.

7. The number '21' is there in the matrix as a red herring. If the general consensus is that the story is of both large complexity and large grunt, then in my experience the story isn't truly understood or it's just too big and needs to be broken down. In this case, the team should collectively break off a part of the story that they believe can realistically be achieved and create a new story from it. The original story, minus the part of it that will be developed, can go back into the backlog and be refined by the product owner and business analyst.

The story point matrix seems to be an elegant and simple way for development team members to assess a story. The traditional way of assessing story points is to review a story in the context of another story. Is this story more or less the size of that story? Is it bigger or smaller? But people often struggle with this, and I suspect it's because it can be too abstract. Getting team members to think about the complexity and the grunt and then read off a matrix is much easier, much quicker and, in my experience, produces fairly accurate estimates.

I'm often asked why I only use five numbers, in the Fibonacci scale (1, 3, 5, 8 and 21), for story points. In his book *Future Shock*,[19] Alvin Toffler first coined the term 'Overchoice'. 'Overchoice' refers to the cognitive process in which people find it difficult to make a decision when faced with too many options; it's a kind of analysis paralysis. If you have story points on a scale of one to 100, team members therefore find it difficult to make an estimate. During planning poker, so many variations are raised that most of the time is spent just analysing the numbers; hence, planning sessions that can take hours with little end product. It's unnecessary work which does not lead to quick results. Use the story point matrix to quickly cut through story planning and generate accurate estimates.

---

19 A Toffler, *Future Shock* (1970, Random House).

User stories – best practice

One of the most discussed and written-about topics from an agile perspective must surely be user stories. I guess that's to be expected as they form the basis for all the actual work that the development team does. Poor user stories, vaguely described, and therefore open to a myriad of interpretations, can waste hours of precious development time. On the flipside, well-constructed stories which open up good debate between the users, customer and development team can propel rapid development whilst creating a system that delivers business value and that people truly love to use.

Assuming that you're familiar with the basics of story writing (and if you're not, you should be), I'm going to give you some best-practice advice that's served me very well over the years. These are simple, guiding principles which will help you tremendously in producing elegant, usable stories.

A story is only a discussion placeholder

Whilst agile isn't exactly new – the *Agile Manifesto* was signed in February 2001 – most people in the IT industry will be transitioning to agile from more traditional software methodologies, and most noticeably from waterfall. Consequently, they tend to think of stories in the same way as detailed requirements, describing the minutiae of variations, acceptance criteria, test conditions, etc. As one of the twelve principles of agile software clearly states: 'The most efficient and effective method of conveying information to and within a development team is face-to-face conversation.'[20] In other words, talking is much better than writing documents or detailed stories.

We seem to have lost the basic premise behind an agile story, which is that stories are merely 'place-holders for a discussion'. The classic story format 'As a... I want... so that...' is perfect for capturing the essence of a feature in readiness for a discussion with the development team. Review your MVP map and pay careful attention to the what and the how sections as these are your stories and points of discussion. Initially, simply write out a story card for each one; these can be further broken down after discussion with the development team. Pre-planning is an excellent opportunity to do this where the development team can advise on the granularity of stories and how larger stories can be broken down into manageable, deliverable pieces of work.

Now, I'm not saying that stories can't have rich detail, but the development team can add this as the story is played out and discussed. Just don't try to do their job for them up front. Let the team ask the users/product owners all the questions they feel are relevant to

---

20 Agile Alliance, '12 Principles Behind The Agile Manifesto' (accessed January 2019). www.agilealliance.org/ agile101/12-principles-behind-the-agile-manifesto

the story, and then let them add the detail and notes that they need to develop the functionality required to deliver the story.

What's the problem you're trying to solve?

It's very easy for the users and product owners to detail exactly what it is they want the specific feature to do. They use the software every day and understand it fully, so of course they know exactly how the feature should be implemented.

But do they really? Users tend to describe exactly how they want a feature to work: 'We need a drop-down here and when you click on your selection a button pops up over here and then you...'. What they tend not to do is step back from the actual implementation and ask why. So ask them directly: What's the business problem they're trying to solve? It may well be that the way they've described their solution is the best way to solve a specific problem. And it may well not. There will be lots of richness that the development team can bring to a solution to a specific problem, so why rob them of that opportunity to add great value? Take a step back, articulate the problem at hand and then discuss the root cause. By doing this you'll often find a simpler, more elegant solution that will fully address the problem, or even introduce a new opportunity.

Think of stories in the context of behaviour change

Sometimes it's better to come at problems to be solved from left field. Rather than think of stories as features that do this or that, think about what behaviour change you're trying to bring about. Essentially, features either change users' existing behaviour or enable new behaviours. Ask what change in behaviour you want to bring about and why. What new behaviour do you want users to exhibit? In his excellent book *The Power of Habit*,[21] Charles Duhigg describes habit – or, for our purposes, behaviour – as consisting of a cue, a routine and then a reward. If you want users to perform some specific action then think about how the story implements this process. What's the cue for the user, what routine do they have to do and what's the reward at the end, in the form of some desired outcome they may have? Thinking about stories through this lens opens up a whole new way to look at solutions and delivering value to users and the business.

Also, a behavioural change is very measurable. You can record how many times a user clicks a certain button or answers a particular call to action. Consequently, you can accurately measure how effective your solution is when implemented and pivot or change if it's not producing the desired results.

---

21 Charles Duhigg, *The Power Of Habit: Why we do what we do in life and business* (2014, Random House).

Ask 'How will we demo this?'

As we'll discuss at length in the Show section of this book, teams don't generally put as much thought into their end-of-sprint demonstrations as they should do. Demonstrations – or 'show-and-tells', as they're often referred to – are the pinnacle of a sprint and a chance to show users, stakeholders and others all the excellent work that's been done in the sprint.

When defining stories, ask the simple question: 'How will we demonstrate this?' Asking this question has two important consequences. Firstly, it raises demonstrations into everyone's awareness right at the start of the sprint, which is always a good thing. Secondly, often thinking about how you will demonstrate a particular story/feature helps with defining an elegant solution, and it helps you to think about how to solve the problem too. In order to answer that question you have to put yourself in the shoes of your user and walk through the solution in your head. When you do this, the solution either feels right or it doesn't quite seem to fit. It's a very useful exercise to go through.

As a... I want to... so that... which means (= business value)

Here's a neat little trick I use to great effect when trying to extract the business value of a story from the product owner. To the normal 'As a... I want to... so that...' story template, ask the product owner or user to add 'which means…' onto the end. Doing this forces them to address the why of what they're requesting. In their why is the real business value and purpose behind the story. It's incredibly important to know the why behind a story as the development team think about the implementation. It greatly impacts the effectiveness of any given solution and helps them make informed decisions as the feature is developed.

Also, if there is no strong business value associated with a story then this begs the question, 'Why are we bothering?' Is there something else we can do with the development time to add greater value and solve more pressing problems that users may have? Getting the product owner or users to answer this question helps them with their reflection. It may well be that a particular story is really a pet feature of theirs that they've seen elsewhere and want to emulate. Some self-reflection by the product owner here is a sobering exercise and helps them make a more detached, informed decision. They may well even decide that yes, it is a pet feature, but they still want it anyway. And to me, that's fine. If they're the product owner and they're paying for it then they can have whatever they want. It's still important that they go through this exercise to know their own motivations.

Conditions of satisfaction

After a long debate over lunch some time ago with Mike Cohn (agile guru, author of several famous agile books, including *User Stories Applied*,[22] and founder of Mountain Goat software), I started adding conditions of satisfaction to user stories. Mike describes 'conditions of satisfaction' as what must be true for a story to be considered done.

Over time I've come to use conditions of satisfaction slightly differently than Mike does. I use them to answer the question, 'With this particular story, how will we know when we've successfully implemented it?' Therefore, conditions of satisfaction also enable me to emphatically answer the question, 'Are we done here?' They're like a tick-box list of requirements that the implementation of the story must fulfil in order for me to know that we've delivered the required business value. Be careful and judicious here, however, and try not to have more than three conditions. It's easy for everyone to get carried away and produce a wish list of things rather than a concise set of conditions of satisfaction that empower and advise the development team.

The daily stand-up

The daily stand-up is probably the most abused of all agile rituals. The purpose of the daily stand-up is to bring all team members up to date, foster team collaboration, and quickly raise any impediments and blockers. That's it. It should take no more than ten minutes

---

22 Mike Cohn, *User Stories Applied* (2004, Addison-Wesley).

and engage every member of the team. However, most stand-ups take far too long, are tediously boring, achieve very little and eat into precious development time. Here are my top tips for running quick, effective stand-ups.

Don't ask 'What did you do?'

The traditional questions asked of each team member at stand-ups are: 'What did you do yesterday?', 'What are you going to do today?' and 'Do you have any blockers?' Do not ask the first two of these questions. If you ask people what they did, they feel compelled to give you a running commentary of their day: 'Well, in the morning we had a meeting with so and so and discussed stuff, then we had another meeting and discussed more stuff. Then we went for coffee with some people from the product line and we discussed even more stuff.' Who cares?

What we want to know is what each team member actually *achieved* in relation to what the team has committed to delivering in planning. There's also a domino effect to this. If one team member gives you a running commentary then the next person does the same thing too. No wonder stand-ups of only eight team members can take an hour. So the better questions to ask are: 'What did you *achieve* yesterday?' and 'What do you intend to *achieve* today?' as well as 'Do you have any blockers?' Asking team members what they explicitly achieved forces them to give concrete answers of deliverables rather than a running commentary of their day. It also ensures team members focus on exactly what they should be focusing on: their commitment to delivery.

In addition, asking team members what they 'intend to achieve today' at the morning stand-up guarantees that their answer remains top of mind when they're making decisions about the day. Rather than just being busy doing work, they're focusing precisely on what they intend to achieve and have committed to achieving. For the individual team member there's a huge personal win here too. Assuming they did actually achieve their goal, then there's a big cognitive and well-being boost as they leave the office.

No side conversations

To my mind, one of the most disrespectful things you can do is interrupt or speak over a colleague at stand-up. It's just plain rude. But apart from that, it wastes so much time. Team members who are speaking have to repeat what they've said because colleagues were having a separate conversation were therefore not concentrating, and miss any questions that may have come their way.

It's the responsibility of the facilitator, normally the Scrum Master, to enforce the one-person-speaks policy. But sometimes people find it socially awkward to effectively tell colleagues to shut up. A light-hearted but very effective way to enforce this rule is to use a Barbie doll or a soft toy. At the start of the stand-up, the facilitator clearly states that only the person holding the Barbie doll can speak and that everyone else listens. If someone starts a side conversation then the speaker merely waves the Barbie doll at them. Sounds silly, but it's very effective. Once the team member has finished speaking they simply hand the Barbie doll to the next person and so on until everyone has had a turn to speak and the stand-up is finished.

Take all conversations offline

Another big time waster arises from having conversations regarding a particular raised topic or question during the stand-up. A team member may have a blocker or raise a perfectly legitimate question, and that's fine. Consequently, a colleague may have an answer or have a similar issue that also needs address-.ing. If the question or issues can be answered swiftly, then that's fantastic. But if a conversation ensues then the facilitator must insist this is taken offline and discussed between the interested parties after the stand-up.

Retrospectives are the subject of endless discussion; you can even buy three-hundred-page books on how to run effective retrospectives. Now, I'm sure there are some good tips in these books, but in my view it's just another example of how a simple, elegant agile ritual of reviewing a sprint has been made to be so very complicated. In software parlance, a simple process has been vastly over-engineered.

Retrospectives

Figure 8.2: Retrospective 'faces'

Why have retrospectives?

As Simon Sinek would say, let's start with the why of retrospectives – ie, what is their purpose and why do we bother? At the end of a sprint, retrospectives are there to review how the sprint went. What went well, what didn't go so well and any ideas about how we could make the next sprint better, improve the velocity and generally make the boat go faster. That's basically it, but for me there's also a subtle psychological side to retrospectives. If carried out properly, they provide a safe environment, allowing team members to be open and honest about working with the team, the customer, stakeholders and others, and an opportunity to generally get stuff off their chest and into the open.

Oftentimes you can't actually do much about changing the environment in which the team works in. You can't change your customer, your stakeholders or the technological platforms that the company has chosen to develop in, but that's not always the point. Most often team members understand the constraints they're working in but they just want to articulate their thoughts and be heard, and that's fine. At the same time retrospectives are not there to be a platform for everyone to simply moan about everyone else and how life is so unfair. There must be a constructive element and outcome to retrospectives. Simply bear in mind, as the facilitator, that there will be some venting of frustration amongst team members and that that's OK.

Who attends?

Who should attend retrospectives? Obviously all the team members involved in actual delivery of story points, but should anyone else attend? Most of the time I'd say no; for example, I'd never have the customer or stakeholders involved as it would defeat the purpose of the exercise. The only exceptions I would make are when the team is working closely with named users or subject-matter experts – ie, any close relationship that has a direct impact on the effectiveness of the sprint and the team's performance.

What a retrospective should involve

To run an effective retrospective, ideally hold it in a secluded meeting room where you can close the door. Take three post-it notes and draw a happy face on one, a sad face on another and a light bulb on the last one. Put the post-it notes on the wall with as much space between them as the wall will allow. Then give everyone a pen and some post-it notes of their own, and ask them to write down on separate post-its their own views on what went well, what didn't, and any ideas they may have about improving the team's output or ways of working. Ask everyone to put their post-it notes under the relevant image of happy face for what went well, sad face for what didn't and light bulb for any ideas. Allow ten minutes in total for this exercise, then regroup around the wall.

Always start with what didn't go well so you can end on the highs of what went well and any good new ideas. As you run through each note, reading it aloud, you'll often find themes emerging, so group similar notes together. Most team members will be suffering from the same issues. Encourage discussion amongst the team, but at the same time try to keep it constructive and not descend into a bitching session. The purpose is to openly air views, to make sure everyone is heard and to keep it constructive.

Once you're done discussing the issues, ask the team to pick their top two or three for which you can actually do something to improve the situation. Discuss the best solution presented, and then it's the Scrum Master's or project lead's responsibility to see that action is taken by whoever needs to in order to improve the situation. It's very important that timely feedback is given to the team about progress on resolving the issue, even if the chosen solution or fix can't subsequently be implemented. If the team gets the impression that they raise issues that disappear into a black hole (along with their potential fixes) and nothing ever happens or changes, then that's worse than never raising the issue in the first place. Keep the team informed, even if the news is not great.

Moving onto the 'what went well' notes, this is great time for positive feedback amongst the team members, some healthy back slapping and happy faces. Feed off it and use it for the general health and well-being of the team. If they've worked hard and things went well, then celebrate it – they've earned it.

Lastly, review any ideas that people may have about improving the working environment, which will hopefully in turn improve velocity. No doubt some things will be easy to implement, some not. My advice here is to let the team decide amongst themselves which ideas they collectively think are good and worthy of trying. That's an important point to get across too. The team can try out the proposed idea for a sprint, review at the next retrospective to see if it's helped or not, and then decide whether to keep going with it or try something new. Let the team self-organise; they're the ones responsible and accountable for delivery.

All in all, this whole process shouldn't take more than thirty minutes, and, in fact, I normally only book a room for that amount of time. This helps the team keep focus and avoids turning the exercise into one big moaning session. Collect your post-it notes from the wall, and you're done.

Summary

The agile rituals are at the core of the agile methodology. They provide the framework and daily structure for delivering an agile project. They bind the team together, are essential in planning the sprint's work, keep everyone informed of progress on a daily basis, provide a platform with which to demonstrate to stakeholders how much the team have delivered and provide a safe environment for reviewing the team's work.

They are essential to the successful implementation of an agile software delivery, but they do need to be kept in check. Just a ten- to fifteen-minute stand-up each day, a thirty-minute pre-planning session, one-and-a-half to two hours of planning, a thirty-minute retrospective and a thirty-minute demonstration will effectively take up 10% of the team's development time in a typical two-week sprint. And I haven't included a single meeting outside the agile rituals here either. That's a very sobering thought. Now imagine what the toll is when daily stand-ups, planning sessions and retrospectives go on for much longer periods of time. It's no exaggeration to say that half your potential development time can get eaten up.

It's the Scrum Master's responsibility to ensure the agile rituals are carried out and to keep a tight rein on their duration. Use the tips and guidance in this chapter to keep the team focused on the work at hand and to drive as much benefit from the agile rituals as possible.

show

NINE

Communicate

'I alone cannot change the world, but I can cast a stone across the water to create many ripples.'
— Mother Theresa

Software development represents a massive investment of both time and resources for a company. It's the kind of investment that can make or break some companies. Software investment is always essentially about the bottom line, either protecting existing income by enabling required cost savings or generating revenues by enabling new product and service offerings. Consequently, for senior executives, CIOs and CTOs at the helm of the companies' IT departments, there's a great deal at stake when they embark on and approve funding for a software development project. That's why they're called stakeholders. They have to get it right.

If stakeholders aren't totally on board with your delivery and don't have faith and trust in the development team, then they'll naturally want to pore over every element of the project and see the minutiae. Ultimately, their heads are on the block if it goes wrong.

Despite this, one of the most poorly implemented elements of a project is often communications. We're primarily concerned here with communications within the development team and, more importantly, the business and wider organisation. What always amazes me about organisational comms isn't the lack of it but rather the abundance of it. Yet no matter how much comms a project produces, there seems to be a voracious appetite for even more. Why is that?

In his 2015 report analysing the 'appalling rate of IT project failures', Darryl Carlton, Research Director at Gartner, commented that, 'When a project fails, the usual suspects are trotted out and paraded as the solution to this latest disaster – more governance, improved stakeholder engagement and better and more frequent reporting'. Carlton concludes: 'Where there are more people or committees demanding an ever-increasing volume of reports[…] there are bound to be problems'.[23]

---

23 Susan Moore, 'IT Projects Need Less Complexity, Not More Governance' (July 2015). www.gartner.com/smarterwithgartner/ it-projects-need-less-complexity-not-more-governance

Trust

How does an ever-increasing number of communications in the form of reports, charts and other media add to a project's failure? I suspect there are several reasons which boil down to the fact that the communications being produced don't answer the business's primary concern – ie, is everything on track or do we need to do anything? If the business isn't pacified and consequently doesn't have faith and trust in the development team, then people will naturally demand more information. Hence the ever-increasing demand for more and more reports, which takes time and diverts huge resources away from the project itself.

There's a knock-on effect here from a human perspective too. This constant need for more and more information leads to micro management of the development team. The team are going to quickly realise that and come to the natural conclusion that the business doesn't trust them. And that's exactly how I opened this book with the man-in-the-balloon joke. Only far from being simply a joke, it's a damaging reality. If your development team believes that the business doesn't trust and believe in them, then all kinds of barriers go up. If you believe your customer doesn't trust you, then why would you shoot for the stars when estimating and planning your work? What's the point? Better to play it safe and give yourself plenty of wiggle room in case things go wrong; hence, the amount of work that the team commits to is naturally low. If you don't create an environment of trust, how can you expect people to put their necks out?

If your development team makes a good first impression on stakeholders, their belief and trust in the team starts positively, and they will inevitably look for subsequent evidence to reinforce that belief. (See Chapter 10 for how this 'confirmation bias' mechanism works.)

I believe that in order to win the hearts and minds of your stakeholders and the business at large there are two important things you have to get right: demonstrations and a report I created called the 'one-pager'. Nail these two, and you'll instantly build trust and respect from the business. In this final section to the book, I will detail how to do just that. So let's crack on, firstly, with how to give a compelling demonstration.

TEN

How To Give Demonstrations That Rock

'Whether you think you can, or you think you can't, you're probably right.'

— Henry Ford

The end-of-sprint review meeting (aka, the demo) is probably the most important, and often overlooked, of the agile rituals. In my experience, teams don't put anywhere near the amount of effort and thought that they should do into demos, often regarding them more as a nuisance. In this chapter, I'll illustrate why demos should be at the forefront of everything you do, including planning, and furnish you with a simple, easy-to-follow template with which you'll be able to give show-stopping demos that will delight your stakeholders.

Demos and confirmation bias

In his groundbreaking book *Thinking, Fast And Slow*,[24] Nobel-prize-winner Daniel Kahneman talks about the various cognitive biases we humans display. One of the biases, called 'confirmation bias', means that at a below-conscious level our brains search for information that supports what we believe to be true and we actively discard evidence to the contrary. Ever had the experience of trying to convince someone of something where you provide blatant evidence right in front of them but they still won't agree? That's confirmation bias at work. The worst thing about it is that confirmation bias is nearly impossible to consciously avoid. You need to step back and get a third person whom you really trust to shake you out of it. That's difficult to consciously do.

I suspect this is why first impressions are so important. First impressions shape people's original beliefs, and if the original belief is a positive one then confirmation bias works in your favour and not against you.

The best way to set up a powerful initial impression is with a rocking first demo and all subsequent demos. This is why I believe demos to be so important and why they deserve all the effort the team puts into them. Obviously you need something solid to demo, but we'll get to that later in this chapter. The key

---

24 D Kahneman, *Thinking, Fast and Slow* (2011, Farrar, Straus and Giroux).

takeaway is: deliver a great demo, wow your audience and everything else down the line with regards to stakeholders becomes easier. You build up incredible faith and trust in the development team – so much so that later when you have to deliver bad news, it's OK. Your stakeholders, users and other audience members are so bought-in that they trust you implicitly and know that you'll get over any hurdles to delivery.

Now can you imagine the opposite scenario, which is what I see from a lot of development teams? Very little is done with regards to demo preparation, and there's no clear direction or thought about what is actually going to be demoed and the user journey or experience involved. The demo breaks because it wasn't properly tested and prepared on various devices – even the display screens or projectors aren't working properly. The whole thing is a disaster, the development teams look embarrassed and the stakeholders and users are left with a far-less-than-favourable belief and feeling about the development team's hard work.

Why would the development team work hard over an iteration or sprint and then not provide themselves with the best platform to show all that good work and bring their stakeholders on board? That just doesn't make any sense to me at all. Worst of all, the development team has potentially instilled the belief in their stakeholders that they don't know what they're doing and can't deliver. Now that may well be far from the truth, but that's the first impression they've set up. That's not where they want to be.

Given that we don't want our development teams to be in that position, let's look at a simple-yet-powerful template for a demo and some key dos and don'ts.

Demo template

There's a great deal of debate regarding whether or not you should have a slide deck at a demo. Many agile books and blog posts suggest that you don't need slide decks and that they're in fact detrimental. Personally, I don't share that opinion and always use a slide deck to introduce the demo. I agree that slides should be kept to an absolute minimum, but I think they're important to set the scene and to reinforce central messages. Whatever you do, don't have several bullet points and reams of text on slides, just the distilled, key messages, headlined only. The bullet points are for the presenter to deliver – they're not supposed to be for the audience to read themselves.

Here are the only slides I would have, along with some explanatory notes about each one:

Slide 1 – The MVPS

Start every demo with a slide that reiterates your MVPS. I cannot stress how important this is. Restating your MVPS at the start of every demo creates a constant and consistent frame of reference for your audience. Every time you do this you're saying, 'This is why we're here and this is what we're doing'. That message primes the audience and forces their brains to focus on the commonly agreed why, meaning no one gets distracted or deviates from the original plan.

Slide 2 – Sprint goal

Listing the sprint goal highlights to the audience what the development team set out to do. The sprint goal should clearly link back to the MVPS and convey to the audience how you're delivering the MVPS sprint by sprint.

Slide 3 – What's on show today (optional)

This slide is not always necessary, but it can be useful to explain in advance what the audience is going to see. Use this slide to give some background or prior knowledge you want your audience to have before the demo. You might demo a particular user journey or only a part of it if it isn't finished yet. If the user journey is not yet complete it's important to highlight this so your audience is forewarned, otherwise they'll only raise it themselves during the demo if you haven't made this clear. It's also a good way to get your audience excited about what they're about to see.

Give the demo at this point. Then after the demo, a final slide...

Slide 4 – Sprint schedule

Finish the demo by displaying a slide that explains what the development team is going to do in the next sprint. It's easiest to reuse your sprint schedule here and simply highlight the next sprint dates.

By following this template you're sending out a very clear and simple message to your audience: 'This is why we're here (MVPS), this is what we promised to do (sprint goal), here's the proof that we actually did it (the demo) and this is what we're promising to do next (sprint schedule)'. Repeated sprint after sprint, this is a profoundly simple, yet powerful, formula that's guaranteed to win the hearts and minds of your stakeholders, users and the wider business community. After two or three sprint demos, no one from the business will be asking for detailed reports and they won't want to micro manage the team. Instead they'll have total faith in the development team's ability to deliver and will only be offering help and support to them.

As for the development team, a good strong demo with a happy and appreciative audience is a massive confidence booster. Everybody feels good about themselves, their work and the project at large. I mentioned earlier that I always hold the planning session for the next sprint right after a great demo. This is simply because everyone's in a positive mood, everyone's upbeat about the next sprint's delivery and they want to re-experience that great feeling that comes with a really good demo. It's important to build and capitalise on that feeling of well-being amongst the team.

Demo best practice
Ensure they're well attended

Make every effort to ensure that demos are well attended by the stakeholders, users and wider business community. Send out invites early, make sure the demos are always on the same day of the week and at the same time of day, and follow up a couple of days prior with proposed attendees to ensure their participation. There's nothing worse and more demoralising to the development team than a poorly attended demo. Obviously we appreciate that senior stakeholders are time starved, but consistent poor attendance sends out a very clear message that they don't really care about the project or that they consider other things to be more important. It's good to point out – diplomatically, of course – that if the stakeholders aren't passionate about the project, how can they reasonably expect the development team to be?

Slick slides

Keep the slide deck to the absolute minimum, following the template above. Put three to five key messages maximum on each slide in large font, headlines only. Also, get your designer or graphics person to make good-quality, professional-looking slides. It's important to spend time on them and get them right. Remember, the audience will judge your work on the slides too. If they look amateurish then the logical conclusion in their minds is that the development team's work is also going to be amateurish. Once you've built a good-quality slide deck and you're using the template above, then there's very little effort required in each sprint to add the detail for each demo.

Rehearse

Set aside thirty minutes to an hour the day before the demo to define precisely what you're going to demo, and run through it a few times. Make sure all the tech works and that you've got the right leads for displays, backup environments in case a laptop dies, etc. It never ceases to amaze me how these simple little things are so often overlooked and the huge negative impact they have. Bullet point on index cards the user journey(s) you're going to demo and their running order. Demos can be nerve-racking for some people who are not used to doing them. Having written out index cards is a great way to control nerves and give people more confidence when doing the demo for real. Running through it a few times is essential in calming people down and boosting their confidence.

Keep the back end behind the scenes

Unless your audience is made up exclusively of highly technical people (ie, other developers), don't demo back-end functionality. Your audience just won't get it; they'll feel confused and wonder what on earth is going on. Only demo back-end functionality if you can find some way of demonstrating it through the front end that is visual for your audience. Maybe you can show some front-end behaviour that responds differently according to changes in your back-end functionality.

If you're going to demonstrate front-end automation testing, then do it once and leave it there. The first time round, your audience will be wowed with automation testing – emulating walking through the screens and filling in fields at blistering speeds is awesome the first time. Then it just becomes boring. No one wants to sit there for ages watching your robotic automation tests run. Make an impact the first time, then demo something else.

The best demos model a real-life situation that will resonate with your audience, especially if it causes them pain doing their work today. Walk through a real-world example of the pain they suffer today and then how their lives will be better in the future because you've developed this new functionality for them. Make it personal to your user community and you'll get a lot of appreciation and great buy in.

Prepare your data well in advance and test it fully. No one wants to sit there and watch you fill in data fields on a screen – that's just so boring. So demo one or two fields being typed in, especially if you're trying to demo behaviour, but have the rest of your data completed where applicable. For those readers old enough to remember the BBC TV children's programme Blue Peter, remember the adage: 'And here's one we prepared earlier'.

Audience participation

Finally, if you really want user buy-in then let the users do the demo. This is particularly useful if you have a resistant user community who like to avoid change and you need a change in behaviour. At the Met Police I had police officers run the demo themselves. It's hard to be negative when cops see other cops using the software and loving it.

The power of good (and bad) demos

I recently attended a demonstration session with three teams delivering different elements of a new enterprise-grade software for a large global IT company in London. I hadn't worked with this group before, and, consequently, I didn't know what to expect.

The first team up gave an extremely professional demonstration, clearly showing an end-to-end user journey mapped in the software, wide in breadth rather than depth. For me, that's a good thing. They also had a couple of simple but precise slides framing what they'd achieved in this sprint and what they were setting out to achieve in the next sprint. At the end, after a round of applause and very few questions, the team members, product owner and stakeholders were beaming with pride, totally supportive of the team and confident that the delivery was on track. Then came the other two demonstrations.

The next two demonstrations were quite dreadful. I won't bore you with all the dreadful things about them, but suffice to say it was obvious that very little thought had been put into those demos. Aside from being somewhat embarrassing for the development team, what really struck me was the visible mood change in the room. The confidence and support was sapped from the product owner and stakeholders. They raised numerous questions and queried every element of the delivery in detail. The sea change from confidence to distrust and scepticism permeated everyone in the room, including the delivery team. Afterwards, the senior stakeholders convened a private review session to 'discuss the implications'. In the days following, the teams were under constant scrutiny, which made them feel extremely uneasy and distrusted by the business.

Now a couple of days earlier I had actually seen the second and third teams' work, and it was OK. Not brilliant, but OK. It certainly didn't warrant the drains-up review session that was being called for by the stakeholders. And this is why demonstrations are so powerful and important. They dramatically shape people's opinions and perspective, for better or worse. Even though the latter two teams' work was OK, stakeholders felt a distinct lack of faith and trust in the development teams.

Summary

You now have a simple, yet powerful, template that you can use for your next demonstration. Always think of that simple-yet-powerful message you're sending to your audience: 'This is why we're here (MVPS), this is what we promised to do (sprint goal), here's the proof that we actually did it (the demo) and this is what we're promising to do next (sprint schedule)'. Remember the simple lessons on best practice, learned through painful experience, and you'll be wowing audiences with Steve-Jobs-like demonstrations of your development team's hard work. Use this powerful opportunity to shape your users' and stakeholders' perspective for the benefit of all. Give them the confidence to believe in the team and the delivery.

ELEVEN

The One-Page Report

'Build your own dreams, or someone else will hire you to build theirs.'
— Farrah Gray

The one-page sprint report was created and honed over several projects (and years) with feedback from many senior executives, CIOs and CTOs. The original premise behind the report was to have all the relevant information regarding the sprint available in an instant, in a format that everyone could understand. I also wanted the report to be slightly forward- and backward-looking, so anyone new to the project could quickly grasp where the project currently is, what's left to do and any other relevant details.

Senior executives, especially programme directors, wanted the report condensed into a single page as they could be responsible for a number of different sprint teams all running in parallel. If you have six or seven sprint teams running at any time, you don't want to be reading multiple-page document reports for each one. It's much simpler to have a single-page document with the relevant information to enable you to sort out the noise. This way you're better informed as to where your attention can be best placed to support the teams who may be struggling or have more impediments and obstacles. Conversely, if a project doesn't look broke, don't try and fix it.

The CIO at the Met Police in London, who adopted the one-page report, asked his five Scrum Masters to print out their reports on A3 and pin them to his office wall after each sprint. This gave him, at a glance, a complete up-to-date breakdown of each team's sprint, velocity and what they were working on next without having to log onto any systems and draw down reports. It's still necessary to have that rich level of data available in applications such as JIRA if required, but the one-pager is a great way to disseminate relevant sprint information to the wider audience, whilst still retaining enough detail to make them immediately useful to decision makers. As Einstein is often alleged to have said, 'Everything should be made as *simple* as possible, but not simpler'.

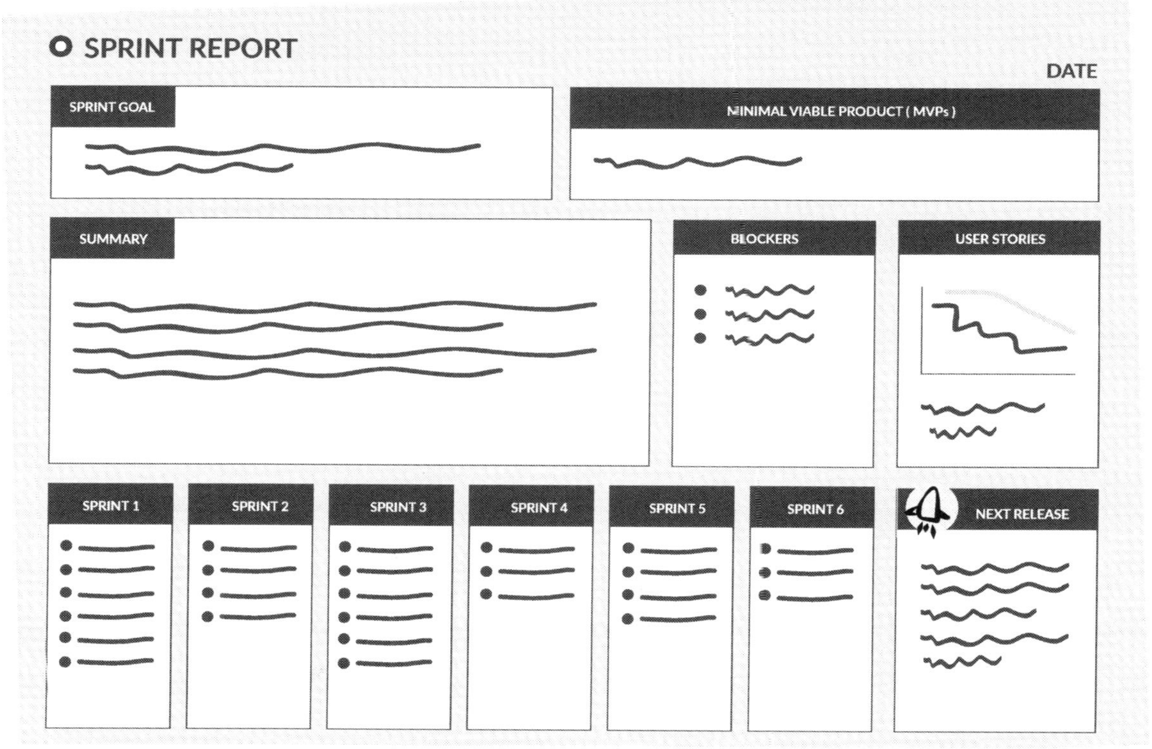

Figure 10.1: One-pager sprint report template

Elements in the report

A sample of the one-pager report PDF can be downloaded at http://thinkdoshow.com/report

Report key

1 - Project name

2 - Report date and sprint reference

3 - Team name followed by report author (usually the Scrum Master)

4 - MVPS

5 - Sprint goal

6 - Sprint summary

7 - Blockers and assignee

8 - User story statistics

9 - Burndown

10 - Sprint schedule

11 - Current sprint marker

12 - Next release details

1. **Project name**

   Putting the project name at the top, centred and bold, enables quick identification amongst a number of reports.

2. Report date and sprint reference

The sprint date is displayed at the top of the report. If you follow a sprint naming reference, such as Scaled Agile Framework Program Increment (SAFe PI) numbering, then list this here too.

3. Team name and author

Always include the author's name in case of any questions and to direct people reading the report to the right point of contact.

4. MVPS

For the current phase or iteration of development, always clearly state the MVPS. At every opportunity we want to reinforce this central message, which is why we always start our demonstration slide with the MVPS too. This is incredibly important as it locks the why of the project into the mindsets of users, stakeholders and the development team. Consequently, this limits deviation of scope and avoids many questions that invariably arise which are totally tangential to the agreed why of the project. It just helps cut down all the noise that surrounds projects.

5. Sprint goal

It's useful to include the clearly stated desired sprint outcome – in particular, what the team had intended to demonstrate. Again, this clarifies the focus of the sprint for everyone.

6. **Sprint summary**

This is the equivalent of an executive summary of the sprint. Include here progress made, what went well, what didn't and key achievements of the sprint. It can be useful to also include how the team is interacting with the users, stakeholders and other key players in the project overall. If there is any disconnect, then highlighting it here will bring it to the attention of everyone as the audience for the report includes everyone. It's not intended to be a name-and-shame exercise but an open, honest point for discussion. Also, it can be useful to add a one-liner on how the demonstration went, how well it was attended and any other essential demo details.

7. **Blockers and assignee(s)**

It's important to highlight any significant blockers or impediments in the sprint report, along with a named assignee for resolution. We're not talking day-to-day impediments that the Scrum Master would generally deal with, but anything significant which the wider audience should be aware of (and could potentially help with). You'll often get people contacting the author after reading the sprint report if they feel they can help with any blockers. Willing volunteers and freely offered help are always welcome. Add an assignee, where applicable, so that person is fully aware that they are responsible and being held accountable.

8. **User story statistics**

From your agile software of choice (or just from your Scrum board), list the number of stories in the categories of 'done', 'in development', 'in testing' and 'blocked', as well as the team's velocity for the sprint. Although it's good to include the sprint statistics, don't get too fixated on the numbers. People can sometimes freak out if the velocity has dropped by a single point, which isn't helpful. Use the statistics to gauge trends over time, and if you're consistently dropping velocity numbers then it's time to address any underlying issues.

9. **Burndown**

I find it useful to include a visual of the sprint burndown chart. Most agile software has some way to produce these graphs automatically, and I usually just screenshot it and cut it to fit the report. Nothing more sophisticated than that, really.

10. **Sprint schedule**

In order to add a time element to the report, include your sprint schedule here. This way, readers can put a timeline around the project and see what's been done to date and what's due to be completed and when. This adds some valuable context and background to the report, which is especially helpful for new members of the team or people who are viewing the report for the first time.

○ SPRINT REPORT

01/11/2019

MINIMAL VIABLE PRODUCT (MVPs)

Enable small businesses to market local offers to customers via a mobile app and a simple web based registration process

SPRINT GOAL

Register as a small local business

USER STORIES

Done : 9 Blocked : 0
In dev : 3 Velocity : 36
In test : 0

BLOCKERS

None at present

NEXT RELEASE

Release 1.0.1
16/11/2019

SUMMARY

During this sprint the team created the registration user journey and the subsequent operator verification user journey. These user journeys take place on the operator web site. During the sprint the team also carried out research with some local business' who were prepared to test drive the registration process. The feedback was reviewed by the product owner and the implementation amended slightly. This has created a faster registration process, which was demo'd at the Show and Tell to key stake holders.

SPRINT 1	SPRINT 2	SPRINT 3	SPRINT 4	SPRINT 5	SPRINT 6
Setup Dev & CD Framework	Initiate registration	Store user object	Map	Add ability to upload company images	Complete company registration
Setup MongoDb	Authentication	Store business object	Map verification user journey	Automate credit checks	Notify business user
Map registration journey	Gather business user details	Retrieve objects and render on screen	Authenticate 'verification' user	Companies house lookup	Map offer journey
Create style guide	Gather company details		Instantiate verification workflow	Approve/Reject company	Instantiate offer object
Create landing page	Create validation				Validate offer

Figure 10.2: Sample one-pager sprint report

11. **Current sprint marker**

    Highlighting the sprint that the report covers is useful for context setting.

12. **Next release details**

    So that your audience is fully informed, provide the details of the next release. Add the proposed release date, any release version number and any electronic story numbers from your agile software.

Figure 10.2 shows a sample one-pager report partially completed, just so that you can get a feel for the type of contents that can be included on a one-pager report.

Use this simple one-page report template to quickly disseminate information to key stakeholders and anyone else interested in being updated on the project status. The report contains just the right amount of information to be a useful snapshot of the current project status, what's been achieved and what's still to be done, without overburdening the reader with reams of paper. Further detail will sometimes be requested, and that's fine, but not everyone needs the deep-dive information. The one-pager comes largely from the perspective of 'Update me, and update me quick'.

People love the one-pager report. It's convenient, it's quick, it's informative and once set up with your sprint schedule it only takes a few minutes to complete. You'll also find that requests for more in-depth, detailed information tend to die down as people become used to and appreciate the simplicity of the report. All of this means less time spent on 'pointless admin exercises', as an old boss of mine used to say, and consequently more time available to spend on helping the development team go faster, which is always our main priority.

Summary

Great communications between the business and the IT department is pivotal to the success of both and the overall success of any project. Sadly, that's often lacking today. In this section I've shared what I believe are the two key elements of great communications with you: namely, the demo and the one-pager. Not the only elements by far but the two most important and the two most useful. Getting these right can be make-or-break for the project.

You can download a free PDF template of the one-page report from the Think Do Show website (think-doshow.com). Why not try using it at the end of your next sprint, disseminate it to the wider audience and get feedback? You'll be amazed at how positive people will be when they read it, and don't be surprised if you find it on the wall of your CIO's office. That would be nice, wouldn't it?

Conclusion

I suspect by now you've realised that the 'agile 2.0' secrets aren't really secrets at all, they're just common sense. But, as the saying goes, the problem with common sense is that it isn't very common.

The elegant simplicity of agile working captivated me from the first time I heard Ken Schwaber speak. The original agile evangelist took the dry, over-wieldy and unnecessarily complex process of software development and distilled it into a simple, iterative process which involves everyone and produces rapid delivery with feedback. What's not to love?

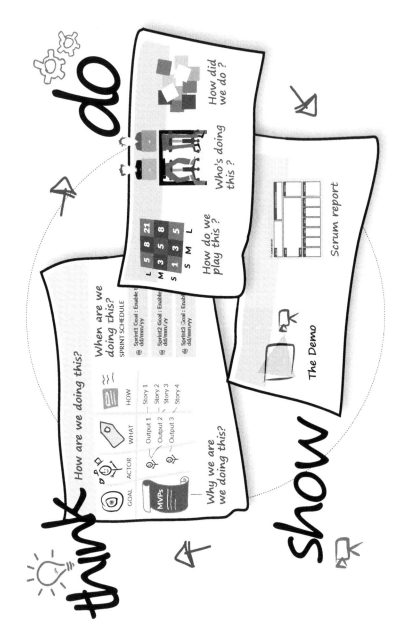

Figure 11.1: Think, Do, Show Frame work

I guess, though, that engineers – being engineers – have grossly over-engineered this simple, elegant process to a point where in some cases it's more complex than the behemoth it was supposed to replace.

Think, Do, Show is a return to basics, a return to 'Everything should be made as simple as possible, but not simpler', a return to our elementary-school fundamentals of 'who, why, what, when, how'. These are fundamentals because they're incredibly powerful and shape our entire delivery. Getting these right and sharing them with the wider organisation feels like you've discovered the 'agile 2.0' secrets.

But the real secret to the *Think, Do, Show* framework is this: the artefacts in each of the sections force you and your team to answer the fundamental questions of 'who, why, what, when and how' – and to keep those questions at the forefront of your awareness, which keeps you focused and in sync with the wider organisation and the true purpose of your delivery. We can summarise this as follows:

1. Think

MVPS – answers the question, 'What is this and why are we doing it?'

MVP Map – answers the question, 'How, specifically, are we going to do this?'

Sprint Schedule – answers the question, 'When are we going to do this?'

2. Do

Agile Functional Teams – answers the question, 'Who's going to do this?'

Sprint Planning – answers the question, 'How much will we do in this iteration?'

Retrospective – answers the question, 'How did we do with this iteration?'

3. Show

Demonstrations – answers the stakeholders' question, 'How did you do this iteration?'

One-pager report – answers the question everyone else has: 'How are you?'

It's been a real pleasure for me to take you on this journey, and I hope you now have some useful tools and ideas. Please don't feel that this process is at all prescriptive. If you feel like you want to follow it all then that's awesome, or if you only take one or two ideas that you want to incorporate into your team then that's equally awesome.

Please head over to thinkdoshow.com, where you can contact me with any questions you may have, check out my infrequent blog and access the free resources that I referenced above. Thank you for your precious time, and good luck!

Acknowledgements

Two years ago, frustrated with what I considered to be the total over-engineering of agile practices, I set out to get back to agile basics. My intention for *Think, Do, Show* was to write a short, concise book that practices what I preach: namely, brevity and doing the least amount of work required to get the job done.

I thought to myself, 'How hard can it be to write a short book with a few diagrams, distilling these easy-to-follow principles? Easy. I'll have it done in six months.' How wrong I was. It took six months just to collate and document my ideas alone. Then I somehow had to bring order and clarity to all this information I had, just to make sense of it for my readers.

After a year of fumbling around, I joined up with my publishing team at Rethink Press. I suspect that no one ever reads the acknowledgments section of a book – I know I don't. Acknowledgments always start off with the author lavishing huge praise upon their publisher, then the author goes on to thank everyone and their dog. I always considered this to be painfully ingratiating and embarrassing at best. Who really cares?

Until I started to write my own book, that is. Having gone through this mammoth undertaking myself, I now fully understand and appreciate the support, encouragement, expertise and guidance given by experts, colleagues, family and friends. Now it's my time not to be ingratiating and embarrassing, but to be truly grateful and thankful to the following people, without whom this book would not exist.

Firstly, I'd like to thank the whole team at Rethink and, most notably, Verity, Maya, Kathy, Joe and Lucy: Verity for helping me structure the book so that it makes sense, Maya for her excellent editing work, and Lucy and Joe for bringing it all together. I doubt I'd have made it to print without you guys.

My thanks to Chinyere Meribe whose love, support and encouragement during the whole process helped me keep going. This book is very much for you, my love.

To my long-term collaborators, and the best software team I've ever worked with, Paul Graham, Dmitry

Panov, Dave Futerman, Pete Hunting, Hamish Keith and Gabriel Osinibi. A particular shout out to Pete, whose amazing illustrations have brought my book to life, and to Paul for continual review of my text.

My thanks to Justyna Cruz of Xclusive Projects who helped with some valuable research.

This book sums up all the practical learning from many years collaborating with some incredibly gifted and passionate people, and it would be impossible to name them all. However, I have mentioned some of these people directly in case studies in the book. I am also grateful to those not directly mentioned in the book but who have equally contributed to my experiences, learning and ideas, including Colin Constable, Correy Voo, Kevin Nickels and Jason Boud from our days at Credit Suisse and BT. These guys helped me learn the art of the possible. To Phil Parker and Ryan Sikorsky, who supported me tirelessly at O2. To my friend and colleague at Hailo Dave Gardner, the best sceptic with whom to test my ideas and approach. To Tom Wetwood, who has provided me with opportunities to excel. To my long-term friend and business associate Andy Dargon, who shared a lot of this journey with me over the years. To Sara Lewis OBE, Mark Simmons, Sue Morris, Jon Butterwick, Jon Philips, Pauline Pateman-West, Jane McBryne and Mike Joubert from our days at the Met Police. We did some incredible work together, of which I am extremely proud to this day. To my colleagues James Bowler and

Simon Morris, who have been truly supportive during our nuclear adventure together.

And lastly, to my dear friends KoKo and Eye for sustaining me with amazing Thai food – and rum – while I toiled away for hours, writing in their restaurant in Phuket.

The Author

Simon Edwards is a pragmatic agile evangelist and author. With fifteen years' experience of real-world software delivery for globally successful organisations, practical advice leaps out in his writing. He specialises in helping organisations build crusading teams that swiftly cut through the corporate fog to ship award-winning software.

Simon is London-based, with a client list that represents a global who's who of many industries, and which includes Apple, O2, BT, Credit Suisse, Thomson Reuters, Shell, GlaxoSmithKline, the Ministry of

Defence and the Metropolitan Police. His expertise has taken him to New York, Silicon Valley, The Hague, Paris, Rome, Pune, Singapore, Hong Kong, Shanghai and Bangkok.

With a palpable intolerance of corporate bureaucracy, Simon understands that it's real humans, working together towards a common goal with easily understood, measureable targets, that actually deliver amazing results.

After witnessing first-hand how teams and organisations struggle with the agile principles, two years ago Simon set out on a journey to show people just how easy it can be, with an emphasis on the practical who, why, what and when. This book is the result.

Printed in Great Britain
by Amazon